Canadian

Writer's

Handbook

Richard Davies | Jerry Wowk

NELSON EDUCATION

NELSON EDUCATION

Nelson Canadian Writer's Handbook

Authors
Richard Davies
Jerry Wowk

Dedicated to
Glen Kirkland

Director of Publishing
Kevin Martindale

General Manager, Literacy and Reference
Michelle Kelly

Publisher, Supplementary Literacy and Reference
David Friend

Product Manager
Lorna Coulter

Project Manager
Maureen de Sousa

Developmental Editor
Anthony Luengo

Assistant Editor
Adam Rennie

Editorial Assistant
Meghan Newton

Executive Director, Content and Media Production
Renate McCloy

Director, Content and Media Production
Sujata Singh

Senior Content Production Editor
Carolyn Pisani

Content Production Editor
Stephanie Erb

Copy Editor
Evelyn Maksimovich

Proofreader
Heather Sangster

Indexer
Noeline Bridge

Production Manager
Helen Jager-Locsin

Production Coordinator
Susan Ure

Design Director
Ken Phipps

Interior Design
Fizzz Design Inc.

Cover Design
Liz Harasymczuk

Compositor
Zenaida Diores

Director, Asset Management Services
Vicki Gould

Permissions Researcher
Daniela Glass

Printer
Transcontinental

Table of Contents

Introduction

Welcome to the *Nelson Canadian Writer's Handbook*! This resource is designed to help you with all stages of your written work.

The opening section introduces you to the key traits, or aspects, of writing that apply to any type of writing.

Part 1 reviews the paragraph, a building block of writing that you probably know a lot about already.

Part 2 looks at the essential steps for writing a longer text—the essay.

Part 3 addresses various writing forms, such as personal responses, short stories, book and movie reviews, and news reports. If you have to write something other than an essay, this is where you will find the information you need to complete your assignment.

Part 4 reviews the conventions of writing, such as sentences, spelling, and punctuation. It also includes especially handy subsections on commonly confused words (see the book pages with coloured edges) and frequently misspelled words.

The **Appendix** features tips for note taking and managing your time.

Be sure to check out the **Table of Contents** and the **Index**, both of which are useful for finding specific information about various aspects and elements of writing. If you're unsure of a term used in the text, just flip to the **Glossary**, which starts on page 195.

Finally, we want to wish you the very best with all your written work this year!

Richard Davies and Jerry Wowk

Talking about Writing

When you write something in school, you often talk about your work with a teacher or your classmates. These discussions range across many different aspects of writing—everything from brainstorming topics, to expressing ideas powerfully, to fixing problems. Knowing some terminology about writing can help make these discussions more effective.

Traits of Writing

A useful way to look at writing is to think of it as having six key traits, or characteristics:

- ideas
- organization
- word choice
- sentence fluency
- voice
- conventions

These traits identify what's important about any effective piece of writing. You'll learn more about the six traits and how they apply to essay writing in the pages that follow.

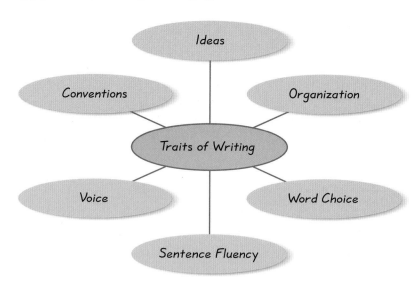

Ideas

Ideas are the *what* of writing—what the writer has to say about a topic. Ideas include opinions, facts, details, examples, and evidence that the writer provides. Here are some questions you might ask about ideas when you are writing an essay:

- Is there a clear topic?
- Does each paragraph have a main idea?
- Are there enough specific details to support the main ideas?
- How might the reader respond to the writing?

Organization

Organization refers to the structure of a written piece—how a writer puts the ideas together so that they clearly and logically communicate his or her message. Effective writers carefully organize their ideas to help their readers easily follow the flow of opinions and information.

Here are some questions you might ask about organization when you are writing an essay:

- Does the introduction grab the reader's attention?
- Do the opinions and information connect well with the main idea?
- Is there a smooth flow of ideas from one sentence to the next and from one paragraph to the next?
- Does the conclusion summarize what's been said?

Word Choice

Effective writers choose words carefully, making conscious decisions to use certain words instead of others. That's because they think these choices will work best for what they want to say.

Here are some questions you might ask about word choice when you are writing an essay:

- Does the writing include specific rather than vague words?
- Are there enough strong, vivid verbs?
- Are there too many or too few words for the purpose?
- Are there any overused expressions, such as clichés?
- Are slang and informal words used inappropriately?

Sentence Fluency

Sentence fluency refers to how the writing moves along. Effective writers try to make this movement as smooth and engaging as possible for their readers.

Here are some questions you might ask about sentence fluency when you are writing an essay:

- Do the sentences seem to flow well when read aloud?

- Is there a good variety of sentences throughout the piece (for example, sentences of different lengths and types, such as simple and compound)? (See page 155 for more information on types of sentences.)

- Do transitional devices help readers move easily and logically from one sentence and idea to the next?

Transitional Devices

Transitional devices are words or phrases that link ideas, sentences, and paragraphs. Here are some ways you can use them, with examples:

To add or emphasize
besides, what's more, in fact, additionally, furthermore

To introduce examples
for instance, to illustrate

To show importance
more importantly, most of all, chiefly

To indicate time
now, later, after, meanwhile, whenever

To indicate sequence
first, second, next, then, finally

To show similarities
similarly, likewise, in the same way

To show differences
in contrast, on the other hand, instead, nevertheless

To show cause and effect
as a result, therefore, for that reason

Voice

Through close attention to word choice and sentence fluency, effective writers give their work a strong and distinctive voice. This is similar to the voice that you hear when you listen to a good speaker—a voice that grabs your attention and keeps it.

Here are some questions you might ask about voice when you are writing an essay:

- Does the voice suit the intended audience and purpose?

- Does the voice stay the same throughout the writing? If it changes, does it change in a way that suits what the writing is expressing?

"I think I've finally found my own voice."

Conventions

The main conventions of writing are grammar, word usage, spelling, punctuation, and capitalization. For each of these, there are commonly accepted guidelines for correctness. Proper use of conventions helps writers to write accurately, making their writing clear to their readers.

Here are some questions you might ask about conventions when you are writing an essay:

- Who is the audience for the writing? Will the audience expect a polished piece (no spelling, grammar, or punctuation errors)?

- Can you spot any mistakes, either on your own or through an electronic spelling and grammar checker?

- Are there sentences that are difficult to understand? Is the difficulty due to a grammar or usage problem?

- Are punctuation marks (periods, commas, colons, and so on) used correctly?

- Is the first letter capitalized in every sentence? Are the names of people and places, as well as the most important words in book and film titles capitalized correctly?

Knowing the six key traits of writing will help you to improve your own written work. It will also make it easier for you to help others with their writing.

Types of Writing

Most writing falls into one of four main types:

- narration
- description
- exposition
- persuasion

Each of these types of writing serves a different purpose. Knowing more about how each functions will make it easier for you to choose the type best suited to a particular writing task. Writers may combine different types in the same piece, but one is usually dominant.

Narration

Let's say you want to tell a story. Narration helps you relate one or more events in story form. It is widely used both in fiction writing (short stories, novels, scripts) and in non-fiction writing (news reports, essays, biographies).

Narrative writing can be organized in one of two ways:

- The story is told in sequence as the events happen over time, one thing after another (known as *chronological order*)
- The story does not follow chronological order, but shifts from the present to the past (a *flashback*), back to the present, and so on

In the narrative that follows, a teenager uses chronological order to tell about a memorable driving test.

> Getting my licence was an incredibly stressful experience. The man who was testing me did not seem too friendly. He gruffly told me to get in the car and away we drove.
>
> My whole body was shaking when he ordered me to get into the left-turn lane. I think I may have forgotten to signal.
>
> I was also really terrified when he asked me to parallel park, easily my weakest move, but I got through that somehow. Then he made me park on the downward slope of a hill. I felt the

front-right wheel bump the curb when I applied the emergency brake. I thought for sure then that I'd flunk!

What seemed like hours later, we got back to the test centre. He took his time filling in the form, and never once looked up at me. Was I ever surprised when he smiled and said, "Nice job! You passed."

Description

With description, you can create a vivid word picture of a person, place, object, or event. By using specific details related to the senses, you can trigger images in the reader's mind.

The following passage is a description of a concert. Note how the writer brings the scene to life by providing details that connect to three different senses: sight, hearing, and smell.

It was going to be a great show. There were long, anxious lineups at the door before the arena opened. The heavy rain had caused some people to huddle in the doorway of the nearby bus station. When the arena doors opened, the mostly young crowd surged in, laughing and chatting boisterously. Inside, vendors at brightly coloured souvenir stands hawked band T-shirts and posters. Down on the floor level, the seats filled up fast. The stage itself looked fantastic with a blue backdrop curtain and all the band's amps and instruments. A long runway in the back and two towering projection screens looming at the sides of the stage completed the set-up. The huge speakers pounded out songs and some kids standing on their seats were loudly singing along. The only bad thing was the earthy smell of livestock hanging in the air. Just our luck—an agricultural fair had finished a week-long run at the arena the night before!

Exposition

You use exposition in writing when you want to explain something. What you're reading right now—this handbook—is an example of expository writing. With exposition, you can define unfamiliar terms, state or interpret facts, present ideas, or give directions. Other examples of exposition include essays about literature or history, science experiment reports, programs for events, instruction booklets, and appliance or electronics manuals.

The following piece of expository writing presents different reasons why some teenagers enjoy drama in school.

Students who take a drama class often say it's their favourite subject. Many students like to try out different roles and identities. The opportunity to become another person or character allows students to escape temporarily from their own familiar lives. In addition, there are so many exciting aspects to plays and theatre: the costumes, the make-up, the sets, the lighting, the sound design! What can compare to the thrill of opening night and the joy of playing to people in a live audience—to entertain them, to change or affect their lives? In the process, student actors may even start to feel themselves changing in subtle, deep inner ways. No other school subject provides that kind of unique possibility: to experience life as colourful, imaginative, and different "selves."

Persuasion

You use persuasion in writing when you're trying to influence or convince people to believe something or to take a particular action. Persuasive writing usually presents specific information, evidence, and reasons that support the writer's point of view. Advertisers use persuasion all the time because they want to influence consumers to buy products and services. In addition to advertisements, persuasive writing includes opinion pieces, editorials, most speeches, and political communications.

In the following opinion piece, a student writer argues for more choice in writing topics.

I write best when I can choose my own topic for a piece of writing. When I'm told that I *must* write about one particular topic, my creative side shuts down. I feel boxed in. Although I'm sometimes interested in a topic that's been assigned, in most cases I'm not. That's when my writing becomes boring. When I'm enthusiastic about a topic, however, my writing becomes lively and worth reading. Perhaps it's unrealistic to expect complete freedom to come up with my own writing topics in school. What could happen instead is for teachers to give several choices, and to make sure that at least some topics connect somehow with teenage life. I'll probably see at least one topic that grabs my interest, and then I'll write something that will grab the reader!

Now that you've learned about the traits and types of writing, you're ready to review how to put together an effective paragraph.

Part 1

Review of the Paragraph

What Is a Paragraph?

If you can write an effective paragraph, you can write an effective essay. That's because paragraphs are the building blocks of any essay. As you can see from this chart, a paragraph has the same basic elements as an essay.

Paragraph	Essay
a main idea expressed in a topic sentence	a main idea expressed in a thesis statement
a body consisting of several sentences	a body consisting of several paragraphs
a limited number of organized ideas and some information	a larger number of organized ideas and more information
all sentences focussed on the topic sentence	all sentences and paragraphs focussed on the thesis statement
unity and coherence	unity and coherence
a concluding sentence	a concluding paragraph

First, let's look at the elements of a paragraph. Then we'll deal with how you can write a paragraph that holds your reader's attention and clearly communicates your message.

A paragraph consists of a group of sentences focussed on a main idea. All paragraphs have three main parts:

- a topic sentence, which gives the main idea of the paragraph

- a body, made up of sentences that provide details related to the main idea (such as examples, facts, and reasons)

- a concluding sentence, which emphasizes one or more key points made in the paragraph

An effective paragraph must also have unity and coherence.

- Unity means that all the sentences are focussed on the main idea expressed in the topic sentence.

- Coherence means that the sentences flow logically from one to the other (called *sentence fluency*), making it easy for your reader to follow what you are saying about the main idea.

Now let's take a closer look at each of these paragraph elements.

Writing a Topic Sentence

Imagine you are planning to write a paragraph about exercise. Clearly, the topic of exercise is too broad for a single paragraph. You can narrow the topic by choosing one particular aspect of it to write about (for example, exercise and nutrition, forms of exercise, or the personal benefits of exercise).

Once you have narrowed the topic (for instance, the personal benefits of exercise), you're ready to write your topic sentence.

Keep the topic sentence simple and clear. It should be an accurate statement of what you plan to address in the rest of the paragraph. Here's one possible example:

Exercise offers many personal benefits.

This topic sentence tells the reader the main idea of the paragraph. To ensure unity, the rest of the paragraph should then focus on this idea.

Most topic sentences appear at the beginning of a paragraph, but they can also appear later in a paragraph. Occasionally, writers will position the topic sentence at the end of a paragraph, if they think it will be more effective there.

*Don't try to figure out what
other people want to hear
from you; figure out what
you have to say.*

Barbara Kingsolver

Developing the Paragraph

After you have decided on your topic sentence, you need to gather and organize details to support the main idea. For your sample topic, the details would have to answer the question *What are the personal benefits of exercise?* At this stage, jot down the answers in point form and in no particular order. For example:

- *reduces stress, improves heart, lung, and brain functions, and helps blood circulation*
- *builds confidence and self-esteem*
- *burns calories, helps to control weight*
- *is fun to do with others*
- *helps prevent illnesses (diabetes, high blood pressure)*

Organizing Information for the Paragraph

Next, determine the most effective order for the points you listed. Looking at the point-form answers to the question about the personal benefits of exercise, you might decide that you want to start with something that your reader can easily picture. That would be the fourth point (*is fun to do with others*). Make that point #1 in your paragraph.

Many readers will likely be familiar with the third item about burning calories and controlling weight, so you might decide to place it as point #2 in your paragraph. Closely related to this is the

Ways to Organize Your Writing

There are seven main ways to organize a piece of writing:

- by order of importance
- by time
- by space
- by step-by-step description
- by specific examples and reasons
- by comparison and contrast
- by cause and effect

For more information on ways to organize your writing, see page 42.

second item about building confidence and self-esteem, so that could become point #3.

You now have two points left in your list, which directly relate to the health benefits of exercise. You might want to place the item about reducing stress (the first item) as point #4 in your paragraph. This leaves what is probably the most important benefit of the five in your list: *helps prevent illnesses*. Make point #5 the last one in your paragraph.

You have now organized the points so that your paragraph will have coherence; your points flow smoothly and logically from one to the next. Your readers will appreciate this when they look at the actual paragraph you write. It will make it easier for them to follow what you're trying to say.

When you are satisfied with the order of your points, you are ready to transform them into sentences. You might want to do this in chart form, as shown below. This way, you can make sure you've organized all the points in your original list in the right order.

Topic and Original Points	Sentences in Organized Order
Topic: Personal benefits of exercise	*Topic sentence: Exercise offers many personal benefits.*
1. fun to do with others	*Exercise is fun to do with friends and classmates.*
2. burns calories, helps to control weight	*It burns calories, which helps individuals maintain or lose weight.*
3. builds confidence and self-esteem	*People feel good about themselves and more confident when they exercise.*
4. reduces stress, improves heart, lung, and brain functions, and helps blood circulation	*The physical effort required in exercise helps reduce stress. It is great for heart, lung, and brain functions, and blood circulation.*
5. helps prevent illnesses (diabetes, high blood pressure)	*Exercise helps to reduce the risk of developing serious health problems, such as diabetes and high blood pressure.*

Remember that you're still drafting your paragraph. If you change your mind about the order or think of a better point to make, it's all right to revisit what you've done and add your new ideas.

Ensuring Unity

A successful paragraph, as you read earlier, must have unity. This means each sentence following the topic sentence should focus on the main idea of the paragraph. For example, the unity of the sample paragraph would be weakened if you included a sentence about how hard it is to find time to exercise. That point has nothing to do with the personal benefits of exercise.

In the example below, note how the sentence in boldface has nothing to do with the topic presented in the first sentence. To ensure unity, the writer should delete this sentence when revising the paragraph.

> My dad has always cared for me. **He works as a computer programmer.** We went camping once when I was 10. I wandered away from the campsite with the dog, even though my dad had warned me not to leave without telling him. Scruffy and I were having fun playing Frisbee, and we didn't realize how deep into the bush we had gone. Suddenly, a black bear appeared out of nowhere and went after Scruffy. My dad heard the noise and came running with a canoe paddle. He began hitting the bear across the snout with the paddle. The bear finally ran off. That day my dad showed how much he cared for me and I have never forgotten it.

Now read the sample paragraph on the next page. Notice how every sentence focusses on the main idea stated in the topic sentence (in boldface). As a result, this paragraph demonstrates unity.

> **Teenage peer pressure can have negative effects.** This kind of pressure happens when a group tries to influence you to do something you don't want to do. At the same time, we all want to fit in with others our own age. This wish to be accepted can lead us into behaving like other members of the group, even when we don't agree with what they're doing. To belong to a peer group is important. To go along with whatever that group does, however, is definitely not a good idea. It's important that you develop strategies for resisting peer pressure sometimes, such as learning to say "no" directly. That way, you'll feel that you are in control over your own actions.

Ensuring Coherence

By taking the time to organize your ideas and information in order, you will be better able to achieve coherence in your writing. Writing coherently means that each sentence logically follows the one before it and leads naturally to the one after it. There is a flow, or close linking, of the sentences and the ideas they contain.

There are several strategies you can use to help create coherence in your paragraph. One way is by using transitional devices—linking words and phrases, such as *moreover, next, in addition,* and *as a result.* (For more examples of transitional devices, see page 4.) Another way is by putting your ideas and information in order before transforming the points into sentences.

Here are a few other strategies you might try:

Use repetition or similar words in two sentences in a row.

Teenage peer pressure can have negative effects. This kind of pressure happens when a group tries to influence you to do something you don't want to do. (The word *pressure* is repeated in both sentences.)

At the same time, we all want to fit in with others our own age. This wish to be accepted can easily lead us into behaving like other members of the group, even when we don't agree with what they're doing. (Notice the similarity between *want to fit in with others* and *wish to be accepted.*)

Use a pronoun to refer back to a noun antecedent.

For a start, exercise is fun to do with friends and classmates. As well, it burns calories, which helps people maintain or lose weight. (The pronoun *it* in the second sentence refers to the antecedent noun *exercise* in the first sentence.)

Use parallel structure (two groups of words structured similarly).

To belong to a peer group is important. To go along with whatever that group does, however, is definitely not a good idea. (These two sentences are similar in structure. They both begin with an infinitive phrase—*To belong to, To go along with.*)

Look again at your chart of points and sentences. If you're happy with the way everything is organized, then you're ready to write the sentences as a paragraph. Remember to add transitional devices to help your sentences flow smoothly and logically from one to the next.

Here's what the paragraph looks like with the addition of transitional devices. The concluding sentence is still to come.

Exercise offers many personal benefits. For a start, exercise is fun to do with friends and classmates. As well, it burns calories, which helps people maintain or lose weight. This makes them feel good about themselves and more confident. What's more, the physical effort required in exercise helps reduce stress and is great for blood circulation, not to mention heart, lung, and brain functions. In fact, serious health problems such as diabetes and high blood pressure can be reduced through exercise.

Writing a Concluding Sentence

The last sentence of your paragraph gives you a chance to focus on one or more key points made in the paragraph. It shouldn't be just a restatement of your topic sentence, however. It should reflect where you have arrived after developing your thoughts on the topic in the earlier sentences. Ask yourself these two questions:

- What have I shown in my paragraph?

- Where have I ended up with the topic?

Two possible answers (and possible concluding sentences) for the sample topic on the benefits of exercise follow.

> With so many benefits, exercising regularly is a must for anyone who wants to enjoy life and stay healthy.

> As you can see, exercise offers much more than just the chance to enjoy yourself.

Which of these two sentences would you choose to conclude the paragraph? If you were to write another concluding sentence, what would it be?

You have now constructed a unified and coherent paragraph that features

- a main idea expressed in a topic sentence

- a body consisting of several sentences that are related to the main idea

- a concluding sentence that emphasizes one or more key points made in the paragraph

Now that you've reviewed how to write a paragraph, it's time to move forward to the next topic—how to write an essay.

From Paragraph to Essay

Do you get frustrated or anxious when you hear the word *essay*? Perhaps this is because an essay usually involves a lot more writing than a paragraph. The good news is that essays and paragraphs have similar structures. Many of the elements you've just seen in paragraphs can be found in essays. Take a look again at the chart that appeared at the beginning of this discussion on paragraphs.

Paragraph	Essay
a main idea expressed in a topic sentence	a main idea expressed in a thesis statement
a body consisting of several sentences	a body consisting of several paragraphs
a limited number of organized ideas and some information	a larger number of organized ideas and more information
all sentences focussed on the topic sentence	all sentences and paragraphs focussed on the thesis statement
unity and coherence	unity and coherence
a concluding sentence	a concluding paragraph

Of course, an essay contains more ideas and information than a paragraph. As you'll see in the following section, however, the process of writing an essay is essentially the same as the one you use for writing a paragraph.

You just might find that essays are easier to plan and write than you think!

Part 2

How to Write an Essay

Overview of the Writing Process

You've examined the role of the six basic writing traits and have reviewed the elements of an effective paragraph. Now you're ready to learn about the process of writing an essay. Let's begin with a brief overview of the various stages involved. Then we'll look more closely at each of these stages.

Understanding the Topic

It's important you understand what you'll be writing about, whether it's a topic assigned by your teacher or one you've chosen yourself. You need to know the extent of the topic right from the beginning. What aspects of the topic are you expected to address? What amount of detail is required?

Understanding Audience and Purpose

Determine who will be reading your essay. Your audience might include the teacher, your classmates, other members of the school community, and perhaps others beyond the school community. What is your purpose for writing the essay? Do you want to present facts and ideas about a topic, offer a detailed explanation, or express and support an opinion about something? Whatever your purpose, it should be clear to both you and your readers.

Brainstorming

At this stage, you start to do some actual writing. You begin to generate and list ideas, details, and examples related to your topic. Brainstorming involves thinking about the topic on your own, as well as talking about it with others.

Focussing on a Thesis

Before you get much further into the writing process, review your brainstorming notes to decide on a main idea, or thesis, for your topic. This is the central unifying thought or main message of your essay. Write this down as a working thesis statement to keep you focussed as you work through the remaining stages of the process. You may need to change or refine your thesis as you develop your essay. When you publish the final version of your essay, it will include your final thesis statement.

Collecting and Reviewing Information

Every essay or other form of writing has content. Content consists of the ideas and details that you include to develop your thesis. You can collect this information in a number of ways, for example, by conducting interviews and by doing research using print materials and the Internet. It is important to review this information carefully to decide which of it best supports your thesis.

Organizing Information

What are the main subtopics of the essay you are developing? Write out a plan, putting your information in an order that makes sense to you. This plan or outline will also help to show where you have enough information, as well as where you may need to find more.

Writing a Draft

Now you are ready to write a first draft based on your plan. At this stage, you confirm the order of subtopics and develop them into sentences and paragraphs. This is also the stage in which you include transitional devices that connect your sentences and paragraphs. (See page 4 for a list of some transitional devices you might use.)

Revising

This stage involves reviewing the content and organization of your first completed draft and making any necessary changes. For example, you might need to move a section of your essay from one place to another to improve the flow of your ideas. Revising can also involve adding new material, cutting sections that aren't necessary, or rewriting a passage to make an idea clearer. Confirm that your thesis is clearly stated. You may have to revise it slightly to ensure it accurately reflects the main idea of your essay. Also check to ensure your draft has unity and is well organized.

Editing

Editing requires looking again at such elements as the structure and length of your sentences and the words you've chosen. If you're not happy with these, you should make further changes to your draft. What words can you delete to tighten your writing?

Proofreading

When you proofread, you make your final corrections to grammar, word usage, spelling, punctuation, and capitalization. You don't want any errors in these important areas—generally referred to as *conventions*—to lessen the impact of your written work.

Publishing a Final Copy

Once you have successfully completed all the previous stages, you're ready to publish a final copy of your essay—one that you can confidently present to your readers.

The process for writing an essay is one that you can apply to all forms of writing. It's important to realize that the process is flexible. Don't hesitate to revisit, repeat, and build on earlier stages until you get things right. For example, a thesis statement doesn't become final until the revision stage, so you have time to make some adjustments to it even at that late stage, if necessary.

The diagram on the following page shows just how flexible the process of writing an essay can be.

The Essay-Writing Process

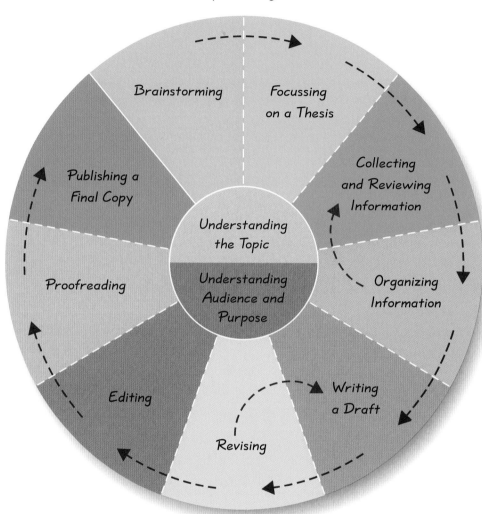

Understanding the Topic

When you start working on an essay, make sure you have a clear understanding of what your teacher expects. Ask questions about any instructions or guidelines provided, such as page length or number of words. Most importantly, focus on your topic. You should be able to express the topic in your own words and explain what it means. When you are developing a topic of your choice, work with your teacher to confirm you are on the right track.

There are questions you might ask when shaping a topic. What are the limits of the topic? What directions or subtopics are acceptable? For example, if you are writing about homelessness, does this mean you're expected to write about homelessness in your community only? Is it all right for you to expand this to include other parts of the country, or even the world?

Imagine you've been asked to write a personal essay about an issue you think is important. In a personal essay, you express your own ideas about something, using facts and details to help you explain those ideas. Let's say that the issue you choose is global warming, and that you work with your teacher to create the following topic:

What can students do about the global-warming crisis?

As a next step, it can be helpful to think of some specific questions you would like to answer in your essay.

- What are my family and friends saying about global warming? How do they demonstrate they are concerned about this issue?
- What action can I take at home and at school to combat global warming?
- What about environmental activism and volunteering in my community? How can I get involved?

Understanding Audience and Purpose

Before you begin to work on your essay, you need to know who your audience will be and what your purpose is for writing.

Writing for an Audience

The writing you do in school is often defined by your teachers. In science class, you might be asked to report on the results of an experiment. In history class, you might have to write a letter from the point of view of a person who was historically significant. Remember that even when your teacher defines the writing task, the intended audience may be some real (or even imaginary) readers you've been asked to consider.

Target your level and style of language to your audience. If you're writing for a teacher, then you'll need to write more formally, following the accepted rules for grammar, spelling, and punctuation. The same is true if your audience is a local politician or the adults in your community. An informal style may be appropriate if the task involves writing from the perspective of a character in a book or a figure from history.

For the personal essay on global warming, you need to show that you're knowledgeable about the issue. You can gain that knowledge through articles and books in the school library, from reliable sources on the Internet, or from documentaries. This factual information is important, but in a personal essay you need to go further. Try to maintain your audience's interest by including memorable stories of your own efforts to reduce global warming. Doing so will help to distinguish your essay from those of your classmates.

To write a successful essay, you should always have a clear idea of who will be reading your work and what you think they expect to see in your writing.

Writing for a Purpose

Think about the purpose for writing your essay. Maybe you want to provide information, or convince your audience to adopt a particular point of view. Once you have established your purpose for writing the essay, think back to the four main types of writing that you learned about on page 6: narration, description, exposition, and persuasion. Which of these would best suit your purpose for writing this essay?

For the personal essay on global warming, you'll probably need to rely heavily on expository writing, because you have to present and explain information about the topic. Some persuasive writing will also be necessary, as a personal essay gives you the opportunity to express your own views very directly. Perhaps you might even try to convince your audience to take some form of action. Including some narrative writing, such as a story or two about your own efforts to combat global warming, would help to make the essay more appealing to your readers.

As you develop your essay, keep your purpose for writing, as well as the type(s) of writing best suited to your purpose, clearly in mind. This will help you to

- select appropriate ideas
- make decisions about the balance of types of writing
- recognize and clarify your own point of view on the material you're presenting

Levels of Language

Understanding your audience and your purpose for writing will help you to choose an appropriate language level for your essay. Here are some useful terms to know when talking about language levels and styles.

- **Formal language** follows the rules of grammar, spelling, punctuation, and capitalization. It may contain complicated or specialized words. It is the style used most often in school-related writing, articles, textbooks, and speeches.

- **Jargon** refers to formal, specialized words and terms not generally understood by people outside a profession or group (e.g., legal and scientific terms). Such words should be explained when they are used.

- **Informal language** is used in everyday conversations and in writing such as e-mails and letters to friends and relatives.

- **Colloquialisms** are very informal words and expressions used in everyday conversation (e.g., *No problem! Get real.*). They are generally not acceptable in written work.

- **Slang** refers to very informal words and expressions used by a particular age or social group (e.g., *wheels* for *car*, *sweet* for *excellent*). Slang is generally not acceptable in writing other than as quoted words or in dialogue.

Brainstorming

When you brainstorm, you start generating ideas, examples, and information on a topic. Actual writing about a topic often begins at this stage, because brainstorming encourages you to write down your own and other people's ideas. For a personal essay, brainstorming starts with what you already know. These are the personal experiences, ideas, and details that come immediately to mind as you think about and discuss a topic.

Brainstorming does require other people, however. When people brainstorm, they often learn more about a topic than what they knew before they started. This process is sometimes referred to as *comparing notes, pooling information,* or *putting our heads together.*

> **Free Writing**
>
> Another useful way to produce ideas and details quickly is by free writing. This means jotting down whatever comes to mind about a topic. It's like brainstorming on your own. When you free write, don't stop to correct or review what you've written. Do set yourself a time limit, though—perhaps 5 or 10 minutes. Once you've reached this limit, look over what you've written and choose what you think might work best for your topic. You'll find free writing helpful for all forms of writing, but it can be especially productive for imaginative forms, such as poetry and short stories.

The initial notes you jot down while brainstorming are usually in random order. What's important is to write down ideas, examples, and details right away—any information that seems relevant to the topic at the moment. As you develop your topic, you'll find that some of these points are not useful or others are needed. You'll have the opportunity later in the writing process to add, rearrange, and delete points as necessary.

Writing is no trouble:
you just jot down ideas
as they occur to you.

Stephen Leacock

An early brainstorming list for the personal essay on global warming might look like this:

- start a bottle drive at school
- join an eco-organization—
  Sierra Club, Nature Canada
- use CFLs (compact
  fluorescent light bulbs)
- buy organic products
- promote watching eco-videos
- "no idling" car zones
- walk, skate, cycle
- take public transportation
- massive environmental problem
- important to reduce your
  carbon footprint

- turn off lights when not in use
- plant trees
- growth of environmental
  movement
- don't litter
- solar panels
- hybrid cars
- too many fuel-burning cars on
  road
- turn down thermostats in cold
  weather
- run dishwashers only when full
- recycle paper

As you can see, you don't need to spend time writing complete sentences in a brainstorming list. Simple verbs, nouns, and phrases will do. Write on only one side of your notepaper. That way, you don't need to be flipping from back to front as you and others generate numerous ideas and details on the topic.

Identify possible subtopics in parentheses ( ), either during or after making the list. The question marks in the following example indicate possible subtopics for some of the points in the list.

- buy organic products (home?)
- promote watching eco-videos
  (school?)
- "no idling" car zones (school?)
- walk, skate, cycle
  (transportation? school?)
- massive environmental problem
  (intro?)

- important to reduce your
  carbon footprint (intro?)
- growth of environmental
  movement
  (activism/volunteering?)
- turn down thermostats in cold
  weather (home? school?)
- recycle paper (school?)

Brainstorming lists can be managed in a number of ways. For example, if you're beginning to see potential subtopics or subsections at this stage, write them on a separate page so that you have room to add details for each one later on in the writing process.

You might also sort brainstorming ideas and details in a web diagram like the one below. Note that the topic is stated in the middle oval, while the subtopics are included in the ovals surrounding it. A web diagram can help you start organizing what's been shared in the brainstorming.

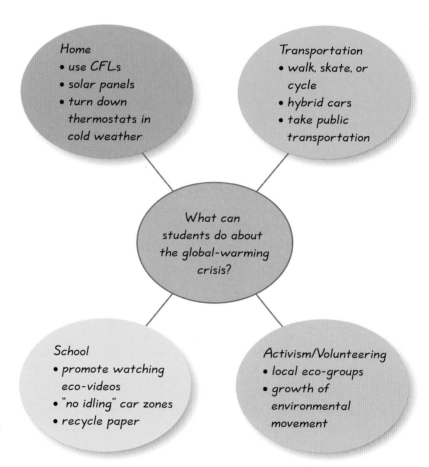

Another way to start organizing brainstormed ideas is to set up a T-chart. Below is a partially completed T-chart for the global-warming topic being developed. Note that the chart has two columns, each with a heading that helps to group ideas. In this example, the ideas in the left column relate to some causes of global warming. For each of these, the right column lists an action that students can take to help deal with the problem.

What causes global warming?	What can students do?
overuse of electricity	• use CFLs • turn off lights when not in use
too many fuel-burning cars on road	• walk, skate, or cycle • take public transportation • support hybrid cars
forests cut down to produce paper	• recycle paper • plant more trees

Focussing on a Thesis

You need a thesis to provide a focus for your essay. However, it's difficult to come up with one before this stage in the writing process. Remember that you must first figure out and record what you already know about the topic. That's the purpose of brainstorming, listing, and pulling together your early notes using a graphic organizer such as a web diagram or T-chart. Completing these steps will help you to arrive at an initial focus on the topic. Writing down this focus will give you a working thesis statement. At a later stage, you can refine it into a final thesis statement.

The instructions for the assignment may also lead to a working thesis statement. For example, words such as *students* and *global warming* might prompt you to write the thesis statement that follows.

Possible Working Thesis Statement 1

Students can take many steps to deal with the global-warming crisis.

Another way to develop a thesis is to look over a list or graphic organizer you created while brainstorming, such as the one on page 34. Identified there are four possible emerging subtopics: home, school, transportation, and activism. A working thesis statement such as the one on the following page could spring from that information.

Possible Working Thesis Statement 2

At home and at school, and with respect to activism and transportation, students can take many steps to deal with the global-warming crisis.

Don't forget that this is a working thesis statement. If you use all of the subtopics, you may not be sure of the order in which to place them, but you can always come back later to rewrite the sentence to reflect any reorganization of your essay.

You might also combine the subtopics. You could deal with transportation in conjunction with school (including details such as hydrogen-fuelled school buses and walking, skating, or cycling to and from school). For that matter, you might also want to deal with activism as a school-related activity.

At this point, a modified thesis statement for the sample essay might look like the following. Notice the addition of individual words such as *effective* and *tackle* to suggest action with results.

Possible Working Thesis Statement 3

Students can take many effective steps at home, at school, and through activism to tackle the global-warming crisis.

Later in the writing process, you may find that your focus is too narrow. In the case of the sample essay, you may decide that transportation really does deserve to be a subtopic separate from school. You may also find that other subtopics emerge as you're collecting information. (See Collecting and Reviewing Information, beginning on page 39.) For example, finding lots of information on alternative energy sources, such as wind and tidal power, may justify adding a new subtopic.

Don't hesitate to revise your working thesis statement as you move forward in the writing process. Doing so is especially important after you've collected and organized most or all of your information. After you add, delete, or move points around, you may decide to rewrite your thesis statement to more accurately reflect how your essay is developing.

FOXTROT © Bill Amend. Reprinted with permission of Universal Press Syndicate. All rights reserved.

Collecting and Reviewing Information

By this point in the process, you will have developed a solid understanding of your topic, your audience, and your purpose in writing for that audience. You will have brainstormed some ideas, and organized them in a way that has helped you come up with a working thesis. Now it's time to think some more about the topic, maybe check a few sources, and possibly talk with other people.

What you'll be doing is collecting and reviewing additional information to support your thesis. As you review what you collect, you'll probably find that some of the information doesn't fit. If, for example, you come across material on preserving natural habitats during your search for information on global warming, you should probably ignore it. Your focus, remember, is on taking action at home, at school, and in the wider community.

Below and on the next page is an expanded list of information based on additional details collected. Like the lists on page 33, the points on this list are also in random order. Four possible subtopics are identified here as well: introduction, activism, school, and home. Notice also that some of the individual points have been expanded. For example, *green roofs* has been added to *solar panels*, and *about $\frac{2}{3}$ less energy used* has been added to *use CFLs*. The discovery of new information contributes to a deeper understanding of the topic.

- *massive environmental problem (intro)*
- *growth of environmental movement (activism)*
- *turn off lights when not in use; TVs, stereos also (home)*
- *use recycled products (home, school)*

- *school-wide recycling of paper, glass, and plastic (school)*
- *drought, deforestation, and clear-cutting—need for more trees and greenery (intro)*
- *important to reduce your carbon footprint (intro)*

- increase of greenhouse gases—carbon dioxide, methane, nitrous oxide—because of modern lifestyle (intro)
- need to conserve water because of shortages; heat waves, drying out of soil (intro)
- turn down thermostats in cold weather—wear more clothes (home)
- turn off computer, other electronic devices (home)
- investigate the work/services of Environment Canada (activism)
- walk, cycle, or skate to school (school)
- solar panels and green roofs (home)
- car pool to school (school)
- use reusable containers for lunches (school)
- shorter showers, fewer baths (home)
- use CFLs—about $\frac{2}{3}$ less energy used (home)
- wear "Stop global warming!" T-shirts, badges, pins, hats (activism)
- give gifts with minimal packaging (activism)
- magazines and newspapers recycled to hospitals and nursing homes (school)
- take public transportation (school)
- natural resources running out (intro)
- don't run stove for longer than necessary (home)
- write letters/e-mails to the editor (activism)
- "no idling" car zones (school)
- recycle old clothes, toys, etc.—give to charity groups (activism)
- post complaints to websites of manufacturers or fast-food companies about wasteful packaging (activism)
- buy organic products (home)
- forward articles about global warming to friends and relatives (activism)
- read a book on global warming—give a book talk to class (school)
- run full loads for dishwasher, washing machine, and dryer (home)
- call in to radio talk shows on environmental issues (activism)
- promote watching eco-videos (school)
- start or join environmental clubs at school (school)
- plant trees in schoolyard or buy plants for classrooms (school)
- join an eco-organization or local eco-groups (activism)
- start a blog on global warming; invite others to participate (activism)
- what can students do? (intro)

There are three main ways to move from an expanded, random list of points to separate lists grouped by subtopic. You can

- group related information onto separate pages, or use a web diagram or a T-chart as on pages 34 and 35

- use a different-coloured marker or pen to highlight or write the subtopic after each point

- write individual points on blank index cards or sticky notes, and then group them by subtopic

Any of these three ways will take you from a single expanded list to separate smaller lists with points grouped by subtopic. The list that follows shows you how this is done for the subtopic of home. Note that you do not have to include every point on the list. If you find that some points support the topic and thesis statement better than others, include only those on your subtopic list.

Create similar lists for the other subtopics (introduction, school, and activism). At a later stage, you'll need a conclusion, but there's no need to be concerned about that part of your essay at this stage.

Home
- turn off lights when not in use; TVs, stereos also
- use recycled products
- turn down thermostats in cold weather—wear more clothes
- turn off computer or other electronic devices
- solar panels and green roofs
- shorter showers, fewer baths
- use CFLs—about $\frac{2}{3}$ less energy used
- run full loads for dishwasher, washing machine, and dryer

As you can see, there is now enough material to develop one or more solid paragraphs on actions students can take at home to help combat global warming. In the next section, you'll learn how to organize subtopic lists into an outline for your entire essay.

Organizing Information

In the previous section, we identified four subtopics for the sample essay: introduction, activism, school, and home. In what order would you write about these subtopics? Obviously, the introduction would come first. Then probably the home section, dealing with a place you know well, followed by the section on school, where you spend much of your day. Activism could then emerge from collaborative activities at school that affect the wider community. You will eventually need a conclusion, but

Way of Organizing	How It Works
Order of importance	Moves from less to more important details, or vice versa
Time	Presents details in the order in which they happen
Space	Presents physical details by moving from one spot or location to another
Step-by-step description	Describes in sequence each stage of doing something
Specific examples or reasons	Presents an idea or opinion supported by specific points and details
Comparison and contrast	Describes or explains the similarities (comparison) and/or the differences (contrast) between two ideas, objects, people, places, and so on
Cause and effect	Outlines what causes something to happen, followed by what actually happens

that will come later when you develop an outline for your essay. Here, then, is the sequence of subtopics: introduction, home, school, activism, conclusion.

Ways of Organizing Your Writing

You saw in Part 1 that there are seven main ways to organize a paragraph. This is also true for essays or other non-fiction writing. The chart spanning these two pages shows examples of each way of organizing your writing.

Example

Exercise offers many personal benefits. For a start, exercise is fun to do with friends and classmates. As well, it burns calories, which helps people maintain or lose weight. This makes them feel good about themselves and more confident. What's more, the physical effort required in exercise helps reduce stress and is great for blood circulation, not to mention heart, lung, and brain functions. In fact, serious health problems such as diabetes and high blood pressure can be reduced through exercise.

I get up at seven every weekday morning. I then have a quick shower, dress, and have breakfast. By eight I'm out the door heading for school.

In the left foreground of the painting is a tall pine tree. Behind that, a river snakes its way toward a densely forested mountain rising majestically in the background.

First, switch on the photocopier. Second, load the document into the top tray, with the side to be printed facing up. Third, select the paper size and number of copies, and press "Copy." Finally, remove the printed pages from the side tray.

The movie is worth seeing. It has a riveting plot, the acting is excellent, and the soundtrack is one of the best I've heard in years.

Both the guitar and the sitar are stringed instruments; however, the guitar usually has six strings and was developed in Spain, while the sitar has up to 20 strings and comes from India.

More cars appear on our roads every day. This results in more congestion and, worse, more pollution.

Now it's time to organize the information within each of the subtopics in the best order possible. Let's look first at the subtopic list on page 41. The items there are in random order. They need to be organized so that the information flows logically and smoothly from one point to the next.

This subtopic section might start outside the home with a reference to the home's structure (the first point below). Then you might move inside the home to look at basic uses of energy, such as for heat, lights, and other electricity-powered items. After that, you could deal with appliances. Water use follows naturally from this. Recycling would then become the last point.

Home
- solar panels and green roofs
- turn down thermostats in cold weather—wear more clothes
- turn off lights when not in use; TVs, stereos also
- turn off computer, other electronic devices when not in use
- use CFLs—about $\frac{2}{3}$ less energy used
- run full loads for dishwasher, washing machine, and dryer
- shorter showers, fewer baths
- use recycled products

Next, you'll need to revisit the expanded random list on pages 39 and 40 for information on the introduction, school, and activism sections. You would then choose items identified in each of those lists and reorder them as you did for the home section.

In the ordering of points for the introduction (see page 45), note how the first two points immediately state what the problem is—its scope and nature. Next, as you would expect, specific consequences, such as water shortages and heat waves, are noted. More general points follow, identifying the need to conserve energy and resources and to reduce your carbon footprint. The final point provides the opportunity to present the working thesis statement.

Introduction
- *massive environmental problem*
- *increase of greenhouse gases—carbon dioxide, methane, nitrous oxide—because of modern lifestyle*
- *need to conserve water because of shortages; heat waves, drying out of soil*
- *drought, deforestation, and clear-cutting—need for more trees and greenery*
- *natural resources running out*
- *need to conserve*
- *important to reduce your carbon footprint*
- *what can students do?*

For the subtopic of school, the first four points look at ways of reducing pollution, starting with personal—and pollution-free—forms of transportation for getting to and from school. Next, three practical points related to recycling on the school premises are noted. These lead to two points related to learning and sharing information about global warming. Finally, a commitment to activism is made, providing a clear transition to the next subtopic.

School
- *walk, skate, or cycle to school*
- *take public transportation*
- *car pool to school*
- *"no idling" car zones*
- *school-wide recycling of paper, glass, and plastic*
- *school magazines and newspapers recycled to hospitals and nursing homes*
- *use reusable containers for lunches*
- *read a book on global warming—give a book talk to class*
- *promote watching eco-videos*
- *start or join environmental clubs at school*

The section on activism explores what wider action students can take to help combat global warming. It opens with a general statement on the environmental movement itself. It then highlights three simple, practical ways students can demonstrate their commitment to the cause. A broader approach to environmental activism follows, with four points highlighting the use of different media to spread messages about the environment.

Activism
- growth of environmental movement
- wear "Stop global warming!" T-shirts, badges, pins, hats
- forward articles about global warming to friends and relatives
- give gifts with minimal packaging
- call in to radio talk shows on environmental issues
- write letters/e-mails to the editor
- post complaints to websites of manufacturers or fast-food companies about wasteful packaging
- start a blog on global warming; invite others to participate

Creating an Outline

You're now ready to create an outline, an overall plan for your essay. With an outline, you'll see all your organized information at a glance. Here are some things to keep in mind while writing your outline:

- Write a working title and your working thesis statement at the top of the outline.

- Include an introduction (for which you already have information).

- Make sure all your information focusses on the thesis and helps to develop it in a logical way. As you saw when you organized information under subtopics, the points should follow logically and smoothly.

- Include supporting examples and details.

- Check for weak, underdeveloped sections. If you don't have enough information in a section, you will need to find more details for it. Otherwise, it's probably better to drop it altogether.

- Once you've drafted an outline, you're free to move one or more sections around if doing so makes sense to you. You might even decide to write a completely new outline, one that will result in a stronger essay.

- Include a conclusion. Before you write down the points for this, though, look over the rest of your outline. Doing so will help you review what your essay says so that you can restate or emphasize key points you want your audience to remember.

The following is a point-form outline based on the ordering done above. Note the use of

- Roman numerals for subtopics: I, II, III, and so on.

- upper-case letters for ideas or points: A, B, C, and so on.

- Arabic numerals for explanations or examples and details: 1, 2, 3, and so on.

With such an outline, both you and others from whom you want feedback will quickly see what you intend to address. With this clear plan, you can move confidently into the next stage of the writing process—creating a draft.

*Much of what we think of as
writing is, actually,
getting ready to write.*

Gail Godwin

Global Warming: What Can Students Do? (working title)

Students can take many effective steps at home, at school, and through activism to tackle the global-warming crisis. (working thesis)

I. Introduction
  A. Global warming a massive environmental problem
  B. Increase in greenhouse gases—carbon dioxide, methane, nitrous oxide—because of modern lifestyle
  C. Agricultural land affected
    1. Soil drying out: heat waves, drought
    2. Deforestation and clear-cutting
  D. Need to conserve natural resources, reduce carbon footprint
  E. What can students do in response?
    (statement of thesis either here or at the beginning of the introduction)

II. Home
  A. Outside of house/basic structure: solar panels, green roofs
  B. Turn down thermostats in cold weather—wear more clothes
  C. Reduce electricity: turn off lights, TVs, stereos not in use
  D. Turn off other electronic devices not in use—computer, printer, battery chargers
  E. Switch to CFL bulbs—about $\frac{2}{3}$ less energy used
  F. Full loads for dishwasher, washing machine, and dryer
  G. Shorter showers, fewer baths

III. School
  A. Alternative means of transportation
    1. Walk, skate, cycle to school
    2. Use public transportation
    3. Try car pooling
  B. "No idling" car zones
  C. Recycling
    1. Suggest school-wide recycling of paper, glass, and plastic
    2. Use reusable containers for lunches
  D. Read a book on global warming—give a book talk to class
  E. Promote watching eco-videos in classes
  F. Start or join environmental clubs

IV. Activism
    A. Environmental movement growing—can become even more involved
    B. Simple, practical actions
        1. Wear "Stop global warming!" T-shirts, badges, pins, hats
        2. Send articles to friends and relatives about issue
        3. Give gifts with minimal packaging
    C. Media awareness and involvement
        1. Call in to radio talk shows
        2. Write letters or e-mails to the editors of newspapers
        3. Post complaints to websites of manufacturers or fast-food companies about wasteful packaging
        4. Start an eco-blog; invite others to participate

V. Conclusion
    A. Lots students can do about global warming: "footprint"
    B. Home and school good places to start—but must go further
    C. Branching into activism: commitment to educate self and others as a way of preventing ecological disaster
    D. When enough people take responsible action, the crisis can be controlled or even ended

Writing a Draft

Writing a draft—an early version of your essay—will give you the chance to

- convert the points and examples in your outline into actual sentences and paragraphs
- add, delete, or reorganize information as you think necessary

Don't try to get every word and sentence right at this stage. As you write your draft, focus on two elements: content and organization. In other words, this is your opportunity to test what might and might not work in your final copy.

Introductory Paragraph

The introductory paragraph sets up your essay and must include your working thesis statement. This is the most important sentence in this paragraph because it states your focus for the essay. Where should you place this key statement? As noted in the outline for the introduction on page 48, your thesis statement usually works best either at the beginning or at the end of the introductory paragraph.

Placing the thesis statement at the beginning of the introductory paragraph is the more direct method. This makes your main idea immediately clear to your audience. The other sentences in the introduction then mention the subtopics in the order in which you'll organize them.

*Writing comes easily if you
have something to say.*

Sholem Asch

Working Thesis Statement at the Beginning

> Students can take many effective steps at home, at school, and through activism to tackle the global-warming crisis. Meaningful change starts with energy conservation at home. As students, we also spend a lot of time at school. What could we do there? We could reduce pollution on our way to and from school, recycle more often, and gather and spread eco-information. Some students might even adopt more community-based practices and use the media to spread the message about global warming.

Placing the thesis statement at the end of the introductory paragraph allows you to take a different approach—you provide some background first and then build up to the statement.

Working Thesis Statement at the End

> There is no denying global warming. This massive environmental problem is caused by the "greenhouse effect," a by-product of our consumer-driven economy and modern lifestyle. This effect, made worse by clear-cutting and deforestation, results in heat waves and droughts. More than ever, it is important that we conserve energy and resources and try to reduce our carbon footprint. Students can take many effective steps at home, at school, and through activism to tackle the global-warming crisis.

Once your readers have read the introduction, they should understand why you are writing the essay and what you'll be addressing in it.

Body Paragraphs

Body paragraphs come between the introduction and the conclusion. They move your essay forward as they deal with each subtopic. Each body paragraph will usually begin with a topic sentence. Details and examples then follow to develop the main idea stated in that sentence.

How many paragraphs should you write for each subtopic? That will depend on how many ideas and examples you have within each subtopic.

Check your outline again to help you decide. Look, for example, at the outline for the home section, reproduced below, that you included in your overall essay outline on page 48. Take some time to study the items in this section and then sort them into categories. Which of these items go together and could therefore be combined into single paragraphs?

II. Home

  A. Outside of house/basic structure: solar panels, green roofs
  B. Turn down thermostats in cold weather—wear more clothes
  C. Reduce electricity: turn off lights, TVs, stereos not in use
  D. Turn off other electronic devices not in use—computer, printer, battery chargers
  E. Switch to CFL bulbs—about $\frac{2}{3}$ less energy used
  F. Full loads for dishwasher, washing machine, and dryer
  G. Shorter showers, fewer baths

Consider using a chart like the one that follows to explore possible ways of paragraphing these seven points.

Paragraph	Unifying Idea	Outline Items
1	Temperature control	A. Outside of house/basic structure: solar panels, green roofs
		B. Turn down thermostats in cold weather—wear more clothes
2	Reducing electricity use	C. Reduce electricity: turn off lights, TVs, stereos not in use
		D. Turn off other electronic devices not in use—computer, printer, battery chargers
		E. Switch to CFL bulbs—about $\frac{2}{3}$ less energy used
3	Water consumption	F. Full loads for dishwasher, washing machine, and dryer
		G. Shorter showers, fewer baths

Paragraphs 1 and 2 might then turn out in draft form to read as follows:

Home is a good place to start figuring out what to do about global warming. For example, solar panels placed on the outside of an apartment building, house, or housing complex draw on the Sun's energy for power and heating. Solar heating is much cleaner than burning natural gas, which releases carbon dioxide into the atmosphere. Some people have even gone so far as to "green" their roofs and balconies by adding plants or grass to cool and refresh the atmosphere. Within their homes, people can reduce energy waste during cold weather by turning down thermostats. People then simply have to wear more clothes to keep themselves warm.

In addition to finding ways to reduce heat energy wastage, there are easy ways for students to reduce their electricity use at home. Lights, televisions, and stereos should always be turned off when not in use. Many modern electronic devices, such as computers, printers, and battery chargers for cell phones and digital cameras, also waste electricity if left plugged in or turned on unnecessarily. CFL (compact fluorescent lighting) bulbs deserve some consideration as well. They use about two-thirds less energy and last many years longer than older, conventional light bulbs.

Effective paragraphs, like those in the sample above, often have the following features:

- They are more or less the same length.

- They include transitional devices that help readers move easily from one sentence to the next, and from one paragraph to the next. These include *for example, in addition to, also,* and *as well.*

Concluding Paragraph

A concluding paragraph gives you the opportunity to do the following:

- Signal to your audience that this is the "home stretch." You can do this very directly by opening with a transitional phrase, such as *In conclusion* or *As we've seen.* More effectively, though, you might pick up on something that emerged as you explored your subtopics. For the essay on global warming, the concluding paragraph might convey a sense of urgency (for example, *We have to do what we can right away because time is running out*).

- Briefly mention all the subtopics.

- Emphasize the most important points you've made in your essay. Do not, however, simply restate all the points you raised. Neither should you add any new information or any details deleted from the body paragraphs.

- Leave your reader with something to remember, usually stated strongly in the last sentence. For example, the sample essay might end as follows: *Students need to take action immediately to save our planet.*

Here is a sample of one possible draft conclusion based on the conclusion subtopics in the outline on page 49.

> Clearly, students can do a lot to help combat global warming. Our commitments to action at home and at school are steps in the right direction. However, we must do more. Whenever possible, we must look for additional ways to get involved and to motivate others to educate people about the urgency of this problem. We have to persuade everyone to take responsible action to save our planet.

After completing your draft, you may find you are not completely satisfied with its organization. Perhaps you need more information for one of the subtopics. For these or other reasons, you may want to rethink, reorganize, or even rewrite parts of what you have previously written. This is called *revising*, and it is the next step in the writing process.

*The hard part is getting
to the top of page 1.*

Tom Stoppard

Revising

When you revise, you focus mainly on the content and organization of your draft. As you revise, pay attention to the whole essay, its major parts, and the overall impression you want it to make on your audience. Make sure, above all, that your work is well organized and the content is understandable. At this stage, disregard sentence structure and variety, diction (word choice), and grammar. You'll address these aspects of your essay at the editing stage.

Revising Checklist

Use this checklist to guide you through the revision stage of the writing process and to help you improve your essay.

Check	Action
✓ Is the thesis clearly stated?	Rewrite the thesis statement so that it's clear.
✓ Is everything related to the topic, providing unity in the essay?	Delete any details that do not relate to the topic.
✓ Are enough subtopics included?	If the topic is not adequately developed, review the information you collected and add one or more subtopics in body paragraphs.
✓ Do you need to reorganize any information?	Make sure your ideas and information are organized logically and flow smoothly. Reorder sentences and paragraphs, as necessary.
✓ Is more information needed in places?	Add explanations, reasons, or examples, as necessary.
✓ Is there any information that is repeated?	Delete repeated information.

Check	Action
✓ Are your paragraphs too long or too short?	If a paragraph is too short, it may leave your reader wanting more. Add information, or delete the paragraph altogether. If your paragraph is too long, your reader may feel overwhelmed. Split the paragraph in two or delete some information.
✓ Have you connected subtopics, paragraphs, and sentences?	Read your essay to make sure the ideas in it connect smoothly with one another. Use transitional words and phrases as needed. (For a list of some transitional devices, see page 4.)
✓ Does each sentence relate to the topic sentence of its paragraph and to the thesis in general? Does each sentence add information and move the essay forward?	Delete any sentence that is off topic or does not move the essay forward.

Revising is important because it allows you to continue changing your draft until you're satisfied with its content and organization. Once you've done that, you'll be free to concentrate on the language of your essay, which you'll address during the next stage: editing.

Editing

When you edit, you focus on sentences and diction. Think of editing as putting the sentences and wording of your draft under a microscope. This is the stage of the writing process when you make final or close-to-final choices about the following:

- sentences to restructure
- sentence variety
- words to add, delete, or replace

Editing Checklist

Use this checklist to help you edit your essay and bring it closer to the stage of final copy.

Check	Action
✓ Are your sentences complete?	Each sentence should make sense when read by itself. If it doesn't, rewrite it, making sure you have a clear subject and verb.
✓ Do you have enough sentence variety to make the writing appealing to readers?	Focus on the beginning of your sentences. Use transitional words and phrases, such as *Nonetheless, Likewise, By comparison, On the other hand,* and *In fact.* Combine sentences, and include sentences of different lengths. (See page 155.)
✓ Is your wording clear?	Consult a dictionary if you're unsure of the meaning of a word. If you select an unfamiliar word from a thesaurus, check its meaning in a dictionary before using it.

Check	Action
✓ Have you used any jargon (specialized language), colloquialisms (informal expressions), or slang?	If jargon is appropriate, define any terms your audience might not know. Generally, avoid colloquialisms such as *No way!* and *It's tough.* If you do have to use such expressions, place quotation marks around them to show you are aware that they are informal. Never include slang in formal writing. (For more information on jargon, colloquialisms, and slang, see page 31.)
✓ Are your words precise and vivid?	Use specific and concrete nouns as appropriate (e.g., *office tower* rather than *building*). Include vivid verbs (e.g., *shatter* rather than *break*), and descriptive adjectives (e.g., *spicy* rather than *tasty*).
✓ Have you used forms of the first-person personal pronoun (*I, me, mine, we, us, ours*)?	Only use first-person personal pronouns when appropriate, such as in a personal essay rather than a formal essay. Don't overuse statements such as *I think that.* (For more information on pronouns, see pages 204–205.)
✓ Have forms of the second-person personal pronoun been included (*you, yourself, your, yours*)?	Avoid using the second-person personal pronoun in formal essays, where you should not address the reader directly.

As you can see, editing is a critical stage in the writing process. It allows you to concentrate on making your sentences highly appealing and your wording clear and appropriate for your reader.

Proofreading

Proofreading is the final step before you rewrite and submit the final copy of your essay. At this stage, you reread your draft to make sure there are no errors in writing conventions: grammar, word usage, spelling, punctuation, and capitalization.

Here are two tips. First, it's always a good idea to have someone else read over your work for errors in the areas listed in the above paragraph. Often, another pair of eyes will catch mistakes you miss because you're too close to what you've written. Even professional writers need and use proofreaders. Second, if you're working on a computer, print a hard copy of your essay for proofreading. You'll be surprised at the number of errors you pick up on hard copy that you don't notice when proofreading on screen.

Now for a warning: don't expect the spelling- and grammar-check program on a computer to identify all errors. Let's say you want to make a statement about someone's eyesight and you write *Her site began to fail.* The word *site* is spelled correctly, but it means *location.* An electronic checker won't highlight it as incorrect or change it to *sight,* which is the correct spelling for your intended meaning.

Whenever you're not certain about the use or spelling of a word, look for additional assistance in a dictionary or in wordlists such as Commonly Confused Words, beginning on page 165, and Frequently Misspelled Words, beginning on page 178.

When you proofread, read your essay slowly, sentence by sentence, and, if possible, aloud. Doing so will help you to

- see problems, such as a need to capitalize a word at the beginning of a sentence or to replace a comma with a period between two sentences

- hear problems, such as a sentence that needs a verb to make it complete

You can use the proofreading symbols shown on the following page when you are proofreading your own writing or helping someone else. You can also consult the proofreading checklist starting on page 62.

Proofreading Symbols

Symbol	Name	Example
∧	insert	The house *is* on fire.
℮	delete	Rattlesnakes are very ~~very~~ dangerous.
∼	transpose (switch)	⌐Raisa,⌐Louise,⌐and Karin are 12, 14, and 16 years old, respectively.
≡	capital	Planet earth may be in danger.
/	lower case	We Ȼompost all our food scraps.
¶	new paragraph	That day ended badly. The next day ...
⊙	add period	Liu wondered which way to go⊙
⋏	add comma	Bring your tent⋏ a sleeping bag, and a flashlight.
⌄	add apostrophe	"It⌄s Hans!" he cried.
#	add space	Daniel#and I are leaving tomorrow.
◡	close space	Chickens can't fly, but duc◡ks can.
....	stet (don't delete)	The pictures are n~~o~~t ready.

Proofreading Checklist

The following checklist will help you as you proofread. You might also want to create a personal list of errors you make most often in your own writing.

Check	Action
✓ Is each sentence clear and complete?	Correct any sentence fragments and errors in subject–verb and pronoun–antecedent agreement. (See pages 155–157 in Part 4.)
✓ Are the tenses of all verbs correct?	Make verb tenses consistent within sentences. (See page 156 in Part 4.)
✓ If you've used a homonym or homophone, is it the right version for your usage?	Check the list of commonly confused words, beginning on page 165.
✓ Are your spellings accurate?	Consult a dictionary recommended by your teacher to find the correct spelling. Also check the list of frequently misspelled words, beginning on page 178.
✓ Are spellings consistent?	Follow the preferred spelling guidelines in the dictionary recommended by your teacher. This will help you to avoid such problems as mixing *-or* and *-our* or *-ize* and *-ise* word endings within the same written work.
✓ Have you used commas to set off phrases, clauses, or words in a series (e.g., *hockey, curling, and basketball*)?	Consult the Comma section in Part 4 for help with correcting errors in comma usage (see page 182).
✓ Have you used commas where they are not needed?	Read about comma splices in the Sentences section of Part 4 (see page 155).

Check	Action
✓ Have capital letters been used correctly?	Check that all sentences begin with a capital letter. Proper nouns (names, titles) and the pronoun *I* must be capitalized. (See page 187 for more information on capitalization.)
✓ Does each sentence end with appropriate closing punctuation (period, question mark, or exclamation mark)?	Make sure statements end with periods, questions end with question marks, and exclamation marks are used sparingly and only to convey extra emphasis, surprise, or humour. (See page 180 for more information on punctuation.)
✓ Have you used italics or underlining for book-length works or occasionally for special emphasis? Did you use quotation marks for short works, such as a magazine article or a poem?	Consult the Titles section in Part 4 for an explanation of when to use italics, underlining, and quotation marks (see page 188).
✓ Have you used quotation marks correctly?	Use quotation marks to indicate special words such as slang and for the exact words from a conversation or speech.

Errors in grammar, word usage, spelling, punctuation, and capitalization distract a reader from the content of an essay. As with revising and editing skills, you can improve your proofreading skills if you work at it. With practice, you will be aware of what to look for.

At last, you're now ready to write and publish the final copy of your essay!

Publishing a Final Copy

Before you begin this final stage of the writing process, remind yourself about the following five items from the original instructions your teacher gave you. If you're still unsure about the answer to any of these questions, check with your teacher.

- What is the due date?

- What are you expected to submit? (In addition to the final copy, your teacher may want you to hand in your outline and any drafts to verify the work that went into the various stages.)

- What page length or number of words is expected?

- If a title page is expected, what information should it include?

- What, if any, style guidelines has your teacher provided for the use of italics and underlining?

You're now ready to prepare your final copy. The guidelines that follow are based on common classroom practices, but they may not be entirely the same as those provided for your course. Check with your teacher.

Paper

- For word-processed essays, use letter-size, white bond paper.

- For handwritten essays, use letter-size, white, ruled loose-leaf paper.

- Write on one side only.

Title Page

- Include on a separate sheet of paper the title of your essay, your name, the course name, your teacher's name, and the date of submission.

- Centre the information.

- Do not underline or put quotation marks around the title.

If you are not required to create a separate title page, put the title-page information (excluding the essay title) in the upper-left corner of the first page of your essay, as shown on page 68.

The Title of the Essay

Your Name

Course and Number
Teacher's Name
Date Submitted

Spacing and Indenting

- For word-processed copy, margins should be 2.5 cm at the top, bottom, and sides of each page.
- Double-space all text, including any quoted materials that are set off from the main text.
- Unless otherwise instructed, align the text at the left margin, as in the sample essay on page 68. (You may be instructed to indent all paragraphs, or all except the introductory paragraph.)
- If you're indenting for paragraphs and are word processing your essay, indent the first line of a new paragraph five spaces.
- For block quotations, indent 2.5 cm from the left margin only.

Word Processing the Final Copy

- Use a single font type and size. Times New Roman 12 point is commonly used and recommended.

- You may choose a different font type and size for titles and headings.

- Always save a copy of your essay to your hard drive or desktop.

- Use the best-quality printer setting for printing.

Handwriting the Final Copy

- If you're handwriting the final copy, do so as neatly as possible. If others (or you yourself!) can't easily read your handwriting, print the words as neatly as you can.

- Write in black, blue, or blue-black ink.

- Avoid strikethroughs and use correction fluid (whiteout) as infrequently as possible.

Numbering and Fastening Pages

- Number your pages. If you are including a title page, do not include a page number on it. The page immediately following the title page should then be numbered *1*. Make sure the pages are in the right order.

- Staple or fasten the pages together with a paper clip, as instructed by your teacher.

Reading Your Final Copy Before Submitting It

- Read the copy aloud and slowly to catch any last-minute errors and changes that may be needed.

- If possible, make a recording of yourself when you're reading your essay aloud. Then play the recording to hear if your writing sounds clear and effective.

- Scan the copy to catch missing letters, misspelled words, formatting problems such as too much space between words, or typing errors.

- Ask at least one friend, classmate, or family member to read the final copy—that extra pair of eyes may catch something you haven't.

The following essay is based on the preceding samples for the topic on global warming. As you read this final copy, keep in mind all that you've been learning about writing elements, such as topic, thesis, audience, purpose, and organizing information. Also note how the essay has been developed since the early stages of the writing process. For example, the introductory and first two paragraphs, as well as the concluding paragraph, are not exactly the same as the samples on pages 51, 53–54, and 55, respectively. As well, the final thesis statement is slightly different from the working thesis statement you read earlier. Look also at how the final sentence has been edited. What other changes do you notice? Such changes shouldn't surprise you. The earlier samples, remember, were drafts. What follows is the final copy ready for submission.

The Essay-Writing Process

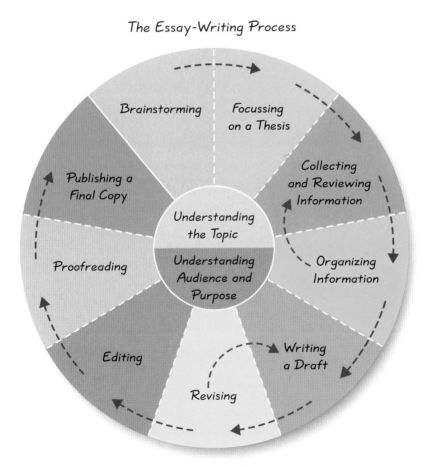

Mira Moses
English 9
Mr. McFee
February 15, 2008

Global Warming: What Can Students Do?

To tackle the global-warming crisis, students must take immediate action—at home, at school, and through community activism. Meaningful change starts mainly with energy conservation at home. As students, we also spend a lot of time at school. What can we do there? We could reduce pollution on our way to and from school, recycle more, and spread eco-information. Some students might even adopt more community-based practices and make use of the media to spread the message about global warming.

Home is the best place to start considering what to do about global warming. For example, solar panels placed on the outside of an apartment building, house, or housing complex would draw on the Sun's energy for power and heating. Solar heating is much cleaner than burning natural gas, which releases carbon dioxide into the atmosphere. Some people now "green" their roofs or balconies by adding plants or even grass to cool and refresh the atmosphere. What can they do inside their homes? There, people can reduce energy waste during cold weather by not turning up their thermostats too high. People then simply have to wear more layers of clothing to keep themselves warm!

In addition to finding ways to reduce heat energy waste, students can quite easily use less electricity at home. Lights, televisions, and stereos should always be turned off when not in use. Many modern electronic devices, such as cell-phone and digital-camera chargers, computers, and printers, also waste electricity if left plugged in or turned on unnecessarily. CFL (compact fluorescent lighting) bulbs help, too. They use about two-thirds less energy and last many years longer than older, conventional light bulbs.

School offers more opportunities for action to tackle global warming. Students who travel to and from school by car might choose instead to walk, cycle, or skate. Public transportation and car pooling are two other energy-saving alternatives that would help to reduce exhaust emissions. At school, students might also campaign for "No idling!" car zones.

Most schools now recycle, but do they just recycle paper? What about glass and plastics? Any magazines or newspapers being thrown out might also be offered to hospitals and nursing homes as reading matter. Students could bring their lunches to school in reusable containers, which would limit the amount of waste going to landfill sites.

School is a suitable place to acquire information and spread the word about this environmental issue. Students could read books on global warming and then present book talks in English or science classes. I'd strongly recommend two books for this purpose from my own reading: David de Rothschild's *The Live Earth Global Warming Survival Handbook: 77 Essential Skills to Stop Climate Change* and Guy Dauncey and Patrick Mazza's *Stormy Weather: 101 Solutions to Global Climate Change*. Students might also request more eco-information in video form for their science and other classes. For example, *Arctic Mission*, a series of five documentaries produced by the National Film Board of Canada, could be used to teach students about the effects of global warming on Canada's Arctic. An environmental club would be yet another way to develop awareness, discussion, and starting points for action. Don't waste time—start or join one right away!

As the environmental movement continues to grow, students may want to get even more actively involved. There are many simple actions they can take to declare their support, such as wearing "Stop global warming!" T-shirts, badges, pins, or hats. They could also send eco-articles to friends and relatives to influence those immediately around them. Likewise, novel ideas such as giving CFL bulbs as gifts or choosing gifts with minimal packaging would help to reduce global warming.

For more widespread impact, students can take advantage of the powerful forces of mass media. They might call in to radio talk shows and send letters or e-mails to the editors of newspapers about the effects of global warming. If they have complaints about wasteful packaging, they could easily contact the manufacturer or fast-food company offenders through their corporate websites. Students might even start up a media blog or website on issues related to global warming.

Clearly, individual students can do a great deal to help reduce global warming. Their commitments to action both at home and at school are steps in the right direction, but these are just a start. Where possible, students must also look for additional ways to involve themselves and others in educating people about the urgency of this problem. To save our planet, we have to convince *everyone* to take responsible action now.

Part 3

Forms of Writing and Representing

Personal Response

When you write a personal response, you express your feelings and thoughts about a text you have experienced first-hand. This text might be a poem, a short story, a novel, a play, a song, a poster, a website, or a film.

Here are some tips to help you write an effective personal response.

Consider your audience.
Tell your readers

- what in the text grabbed your attention, and why it might be of interest to them

- how the text affected you personally (for example, how it connected with your own experiences and views both in the past and present)

Explore and clarify your feelings and thoughts.
Writing a personal response gives you the opportunity to explore and clarify your feelings and thoughts about a text. In writing about a short story or film, for instance, you might consider questions such as the following:

- How realistic or lifelike are the characters?

- How gripping is the plot?

- In what ways do you connect with one or more of the characters, situations, or ideas? (For instance, does a character in the text make a decision that you would or wouldn't make?)

- How does this text compare with another text that you've read or seen?

- What do you like most and least about the text? Why?

Provide clearly stated details in an organized way.
It's not enough to write that you dislike a text, or that it makes you feel happy or inspired to change your life in some way. Your reader expects

- specific details from the text to support what you feel and think about it

- clearly written sentences

- sentences and paragraphs that flow smoothly and logically from one to the next, and express your main idea

In the sample personal response that follows, a student responds to the well-known poem "Stopping by Woods on a Snowy Evening" by American poet Robert Frost. Note how the writer provides specific lines from the poem to support her statements, and shares a memorable personal experience related to the situation and ideas in the poem.

Sample Personal Response

This is a good poem. Overall, it's very clear and I like the fact that it rhymes, unlike free verse. A man, with his horse and sleigh, is stopping outside a village in the woods near a frozen lake. It's winter and "the darkest evening of the year." This may mean the winter solstice. It could also be a reference to the man's mood and how he feels—dark in the sense of bleak or lonely perhaps.

The poem reminds me of an experience I had one winter when I was out at the farm one night skating with my cousin. It was really strange to be out there out on the creek under the stars and moon. There was one point I recall when I became separated from my cousin and was "spooked." I couldn't hear or see her and that made me really anxious. That was too much isolation for a city kid like me!

This man in the poem doesn't seem to mind the same solitude that made me anxious, however. He says, "The woods are lovely, dark and deep." Most of the teenagers I know couldn't stand to experience that kind of quiet and isolation. We're just so "plugged in" to our MP3s that maybe we've lost touch with nature and can't appreciate it the same way he can.

Short Story

A short story is a fictional prose narrative that can be easily read in one sitting. Some short stories are as short as one or two pages, but most run between five and fifteen pages. A typical short story contains most, if not all, of the following elements: story idea, theme, plot, conflict, character, point of view, setting, mood, and dialogue. Let's explore how you can work with these elements to create a short story that will appeal to readers.

Elements in a Short Story

Story Idea

The first step in writing a short story is to come up with a story idea or theme on which to build your narrative. A story idea is a specific imagined situation (for example, *a student is caught shoplifting from a corner store on his lunch hour*, or *a young woman doesn't know whether she should get on an airplane during a blizzard*). Each of these attention-grabbing situations triggers questions in your (and your reader's) mind, such as *How did this person find himself or herself in this situation?* and, as with all good narratives, *What happens next?* The story will need to explore answers to such questions.

Theme

A theme is less concrete than a story idea. It's a general observation about life or human behaviour that you want to convey through a story. Some common themes include the following: establishing individual identity, conflict between people, and finding harmony with nature. You might think of a theme before you have an actual story idea or situation that will bring the theme to life. If you're starting with a theme, write it down for ongoing reference as you're creating your short story. Doing so will ensure your story has thematic unity.

Plot and Conflict

The word *plot* refers to the events that happen in a story. In an effective short story, these events are closely connected and focus on a main conflict, which creates tension that may or may not be resolved by the end of the story. This tension can be presented as

- internal conflict, which usually centres on the story's main character (as will probably happen, for instance, with the story idea of the young woman waiting to get on the plane)

- external conflict, which occurs between two individuals or between an individual and some outside force such as nature or society (as could emerge from the story idea about the student caught shoplifting)

What usually interests a reader most is how the main character in a short story will deal with internal or external conflict.

Character and Point of View

A character is a fictional person, animal, or other entity (such as a robot, monster, or supernatural being) in a literary work. Usually, a short story has one main character on whose feelings, thoughts, and behaviour the story focusses. The story can be told either directly in the first person by this character (*I was alone at the corner of Main and Laurier when* …), or from a third-person perspective (*He was alone at the corner of Main and Laurier when* …). Each point of view requires a different presentation.

- The first-person point of view means that everything presented in the story is seen and interpreted from only one personal perspective.

- A third-person point of view that is omniscient (all-knowing) allows the writer greater flexibility in developing the characters and events in a story so that the reader knows what all the characters are doing and thinking as the plot unfolds. When a writer uses a limited omniscient point of view, the story is also told in the third person but from the perspective of only one character.

Setting and Mood

The setting—where and when the story takes place—provides the backdrop for the plot and is closely related to the mood, or atmosphere, of the story. When handled effectively, mood has a memorable impact on the reader. A story set in a foggy graveyard at midnight, for example, raises a reader's expectations of what might happen.

Dialogue

Writers often include dialogue to allow their characters to express directly to one another what they are thinking and feeling. Dialogue helps to make the narrative lively. Here is an example of a dialogue between two characters who have just met each other:

> "Did you just arrive in town?" she asked, eager to know more about him.
>
> "Just last week and I'm happy to meet you," he replied with a smile.

A Short, Short Story

Let's now take a close look at a sample of a short, short story. As you read this story, note how the writer uses the different elements. For example, the theme is stated right at the beginning, and conflict is evident in dialogue between the first-person narrator and another character named Shannon. Note also how the writer has narrowed down the plot to three events, with the most important moment coming in the third event. This event changes the way the main character sees both himself and Shannon.

Tips for Writing Short Stories

- Read lots of stories by other writers and note how they use short-story elements.
- Keep a list of possible story ideas and themes.
- Use free writing to help get started (see page 32).
- Join a short-story writing group.
- Have other people read your story. Make revisions to address their questions or concerns.

You can find a sample of a short, short story on the following two pages.

Thoughtless

Sometimes you're better to keep your mouth shut—especially when you're angry with someone.

We'd been together several months and the other kids were beginning to look at us as a model couple. I kept hearing some of the girls saying, "You're so lucky to have Shannon. She's special."

And that was true. She *was* special and different. She didn't put on a show like some people do. She was herself and always seemed relaxed. She wanted to be part of my life. Like that Friday night at that big game, when I got to quarterback the Saints in the final. We were getting whipped. Nothing worked. Missed patterns, dropped passes. I was butterfingers, and the other guys were starting to wonder what was happening.

Shannon ran over to me at half-time and said, "I know you can do better. There's still the second half," and then she gave me a hug. That was the first time she had ever shown that kind of feeling in public in front of a big crowd. As it turned out, the team ended up coming back to win the game when I threw a late touchdown.

I guess when you're our age there's sometimes a tendency to tell all when you're really wowed by someone. I remember the day I confessed about the time I pushed my younger brother too far and he ran away for most of a day. My parents were so angry with me!

Shannon had her secrets, too. "Promise you'll never tell," she whispered. And naturally you never think or expect you ever will. Until one day you've outgrown each other—you change, have different interests. The river having flowed downstream and all that.

She had made me so mad by ignoring me when I said we could stay friends after I broke up with her. I didn't mean to, but I told one of my buddies about her secret—the never-tell-anyone kind. "Her dad's in jail. He's serving 10 years."

Boy, word sure gets around fast. I was coming out of the gym the next day and she was waiting to confront me. "I can't believe you'd do this. I trusted you. I never thought you'd … " then she broke off sobbing and ran away.

I was burnt toast standing there, a first-class fool. Stupid, stupid. Why did I do it? It really hurt bad seeing her like this and realizing it was all so unnecessary.

Then it hit me. It would never be the same. *We* would never be the same. We were through every which way now. She had meant much more than I'd ever dreamed, but I had never deserved her. She was far too good a person to be associated with the likes of me.

We tell ourselves stories in
order to live.

Joan Didion

Poem

A poem is a highly focussed, often short piece of writing consisting of carefully chosen words and precisely arranged lines. Poems have other distinct characteristics as well, which are described below.

Vivid Imagery

Images in effective poems are meant to stimulate the reader's imagination, as do these two lines from "The Streets of Purple Cloth" by Alberta poet Karen Connelly:

> *Dragons with scales of brilliant glass*
> *close their tired jaws*

To create such images, writers of poems often use similes and metaphors. In a simile, one thing is said to be *like* another; in a metaphor, one thing is said to *be* another.

> *The busy highway, like a richly jewelled belt, sparkled in the dark.* (simile)

> *A richly jewelled belt of busy highway sparkled in the dark.* (metaphor)

Striking Rhythm

A poem is usually at its best when read aloud. This is because the rhythm of a poem's lines is often much more striking than the rhythm of lines of prose. Compare the rhythm of a line of poetry (below) with the rhythm of the sentence from a news report. Read both these examples aloud to hear their different rhythms.

> *Streets of winter night, wild, wind-blasted, chilled to ice* (line from poem)

> *The wild nighttime winds blasted through the icy streets.* (sentence from a news report)

Heightened Word Sounds

Poets choose words not only for their meaning, but also for the way they sound, using two main techniques:

- onomatopoeia, in which words imitate actual sounds: *hiss, buzz, thud, crash, squeak*

- alliteration, in which the same initial consonant sound is repeated in a sequence of words: **D**eep, **d**ark water, **d**en of the **d**readed Saron

Rhymed and Unrhymed Verses

While other forms of writing are made up of sentences and paragraphs, poems consist of *verses*, which are individual lines of words that may or may not rhyme. A group of verses is called a *stanza*.

The following two verses from the single-stanza poem "The Eel" by American poet Ogden Nash end with rhymes (*eels*, *meals*).

I don't mind eels
Except as meals.

The following two verses from a longer poem titled "Your Buildings" by Mi'kmaq poet and Nova Scotia resident Rita Joe do not rhyme (*glint*, *sun*).

Unfeeling concrete smothers,
windows glint
Like water to the sun.

Rhyming poems usually follow fixed patterns, such as rhyming pairs of verse (AA, BB, CC, and so on); or rhyming alternate lines of verse (ABAB). The example that follows, which is from the first stanza of the poem "A Poison Tree" by British poet William Blake, illustrates the rhyming pairs pattern.

I was angry with my friend:	A
I told my wrath, my wrath did end.	A
I was angry with my foe:	B
I told it not, my wrath did grow.	B

The single-stanza poem "First Fig" by American poet Edna St. Vincent Millay shows the rhyming alternate lines pattern.

My candle burns at both ends;	A
It will not last the night;	B
But ah, my foes, and oh, my friends—	A
It gives a lovely light.	B

Free verse is a type of unrhymed poetry. The rest of this section outlines the process for writing a free-verse poem of your own.

Poetry is where language
is renewed.

Margaret Atwood

A free-verse poem has some distinct characteristics.

- It has no regular rhyme.

- It has no regular rhythm. Instead, free-verse poetry incorporates a rhythm that is similar to the rhythm of everyday, conversational speech.

- Line lengths tend to be irregular. This allows the poet to place special emphasis on single-word lines and on words at the ends of longer lines.

- Spacing and punctuation (which may not be included) are used for special effect, such as to signal a pause or an acceleration in pace.

The following verses from the poem "Progress" by Métis poet and Manitoba resident Emma LaRocque illustrate these characteristics.

Earth poet
So busy
weaving
*   magic*
into words

so busy
placing
*   patterns*
quilting
*   stars*
so busy
making
*   the sun*
dance

Brainstorm

Once you select a single moment, idea, or experience to write about, brainstorm a list of words, phrases, and images related to it. Below are brainstormed ideas for a free-verse poem about witnessing a motorcycle accident. You may also want to draw a simple picture of what you're recalling or describing to help with your brainstorming.

- accident
- cars honking
- red and blue lights
- about five cops writing down
  names

- mangled motorbike
- semitrailer
- black jacket, black motorbike
- blood, broken glass
- looking in rearview mirror

Arrange Images

Next, arrange your emerging list of images according to the order in which they happened or how you want your reader to imagine them. You may also want to add new details and eliminate others from your brainstorming list.

- red and blue lights
- mangled motorbike
- semitrailer
- young male
- black jacket, black motorbike
- joggers and police
- people babbling
- tired cops

- curious drivers
- death and gore
- looking in rearview mirror
- sirens and ambulance
- must get home
- don't want to be late for
  dinner

Write a Draft

Here is a possible draft for a first stanza of the poem:

> Red, blue lights
> blink on and off
> The mangled motorbike
> sputters in defeat
> its twisted metal
> a cruel sacrifice
> to the brutal semitrailer

It is important to make conscious choices about particular words, line lengths, spacing, and stanza organization when writing a free-verse poem. Decide where you want to end your lines to give extra emphasis to particular words. As you write your poem, remain aware of the many alternatives you have to make your poem more intense, vivid, and memorable. Before you write your final copy, read aloud what you've written to make sure your poem has all three of these important qualities.

What follows is a final copy of the complete poem. Notice how the stanzas organize different parts of the experience, just as paragraphs do for other forms of writing. The first stanza and image reflect what you would typically see when first approaching an accident scene. The repetition and spacing in the first six very short lines suggest the flickering of the lights. *Sputters*, a strong verb, stands out in a line on its own. Key words that catch the eye—those that are set on their own line or at the ends of lines—present the main images and the writer's impressions of the scene (for example, *motorbike, defeat, metal, brutal, writhes, glass, blood, vultures, crowd, dinner*).

The last line is unexpected and demonstrates the use of irony. The narrator of the poem is showing he or she is no better in some ways than the other drivers. Like them, the narrator is easily distanced from the scene and the pain and tragedy of the event.

Accident

Red   blue   red   blue
lights blink
on
      and
             off
the mangled motorbike
sputters
in defeat
its twisted metal
a cruel sacrifice to the
brutal
semitrailer

some young male
(no previous record)
writhes
in dirt and jagged glass
his black jacket
blotted with
blood

onlookers gape
waiting
to babble babble to
tired police

other vultures
cruise   by   slowly
eager for glimpses
of death and gore

in my mirror
I see an urgent ambulance
approach the crowd
and wonder
Am I late for dinner?

Script

A script is the written text of a movie, stage play, television show, or radio program that is intended to be performed for an audience.

Elements in a Script

A script has many of the same elements as a story:

- plot
- internal and external conflict
- character
- setting
- dialogue (the characters' spoken exchanges with one another)

In a script, these elements are used quite differently than in a story, however. They are adapted in the following ways to suit the requirements of performance rather than of just reading:

- Plot and conflict are presented almost exclusively through what the characters do and say—their actions and dialogue. The word *action* itself is, in fact, often used to refer to the plot of a script.
- Settings are contained within scenes, which very clearly subdivide the plot and help move it forward. Scriptwriters also use scenes to communicate different points of view, to reveal what is happening to other characters besides the protagonist (the main character), and to provide information to the audience that the protagonist does not know (referred to as *dramatic irony*).

Script Conventions

To achieve their unique effects, scripts, especially when performed rather than read, rely on a number of conventions.

Stage Directions

Stage directions do most, if not all, of the following:

- instruct performers on how to deliver some of their lines (for example, *very angrily, quietly*)
- tell performers how and when to move on stage
- describe how the performers should be dressed
- provide clues as to what the sets might look like
- offer guidelines for lighting, music, sound, and other technical effects

Monologue

A monologue is a long, uninterrupted speech delivered by one performer in the presence of one or more other performers. Scriptwriters use monologues to reveal, in a very straightforward way, the background of a character and what he or she is feeling or thinking.

Soliloquy

A soliloquy is a speech made by one character (usually the protagonist) alone on stage and directly to the audience. More intense than a monologue, a soliloquy is meant to reveal the speaker's feelings and thoughts, especially inner conflicts and motivations.

Aside

An aside is a short comment made *to the side*, away from the main action and not intended to be heard by the other characters. It is meant to show quickly how a character is reacting to something going on at a particular moment in the action (for example, the reaction to the first appearance of another character).

Narration or Voice-over

The words of someone speaking about but not within the action of a script are considered narration or a voice-over. These words provide background information or commentary on elements such as plot, characters, and setting. Voice-over is quite commonly used in movie and television dramas.

Script Format Guidelines

Below is a list of common conventions used in formatting scripts:

- Always start with a list of characters. You may also want to include some simple descriptions and background information.

- Remember that changes of scene will require some stage and setting information in your stage directions. Any additional directions beyond dialogue within a scene should be italicized and put in parentheses.

- For dialogue, write the name of the character on the left in capital letters, followed by a colon. No quotation marks are needed.

- Camera shots and camera angles are indicated within stage directions in scripts for television and movies.

The following is a sample script from a stage play showing some of the above conventions.

Sample Stage Play Script

Scene 2

The same jury room the next day. The jury members enter, chatting in a friendly manner. They sit down and the jury foreperson begins to speak.

FOREPERSON: All right, who'll go first?

JUROR 1:   I will. It's an open-and-shut case. (*waves hands dismissively*)

JUROR 2:   Meaning?

JUROR 1:   Kid's guilty.

JUROR 2:   Of?

JUROR 1:	Of dangerous driving causing death, I say. The car hit nearly 150 in a 100-km zone.
JUROR 3:	(*quietly*) Personally, I'm more concerned about his hitting the SUV in the right lane as he moved out to pass. That guy and his family didn't deserve to end up in hospital.
JUROR 4:	(*chiming in*) Yeah, but that comes back to the issue of how fast the kid was going. He shouldn't have been going that fast in the first place.
JUROR 5:	I think you people are all forgetting something. The boy is only 15. He said he was trying to get his mother to a doctor.
JUROR 6:	That's right. The coroner confirmed the kid's version that she had broken her leg *before* the crash.
JUROR 1:	(*confidently now*) Still, he had no right to speed like that.
JUROR 2:	Is 150 in a 100 zone dangerous driving?
JUROR 5:	(*shaking head*) I don't know how we can pass judgment on someone who is a victim of black ice and his desperation to get emergency medical treatment for his mother.
FOREPERSON:	(*to Juror 7*) What do you say? You haven't said anything since Day One of this trial.
JUROR 7:	(*looking up at the others*) Well, I'm just thinking, trying to sift through all this contradictory evidence.
JUROR 1:	And?
JUROR 7:	And it seems to me the boy had good intentions …
JUROR 4:	(*aside*) We all know where that road leads …

JUROR 7:	And it is unfortunate he didn't have enough experience with driving, let alone winter driving.
JUROR 6:	She's right.
JUROR 7:	(*continuing*) Look at it this way. The car skidded, then rolled on him, and he has been devastated by his responsibility for his mother's death and the injuries to the SUV occupants. He could hardly speak when he got up on the stand.
JUROR 1:	What I want to know is plain and simple—was he driving too fast? Did speed lead to his mother's death and the injuries to innocent people minding their own business on their way home?
FOREPERSON:	OK, folks, looks like we may be here for some time....

Character Sketch

A character sketch is a description and analysis of a fictional person in a literary or media text, such as a movie or television series. In a character sketch, you use specific examples and quotations from the text to identify for readers

- what the character feels and thinks
- what the character says
- how the character behaves and reacts to others and to different situations
- what other characters in the fictional work think and say about the character
- how the character changes, if at all, over the course of the story

As you read or view the story, take note of adjectives that come to mind or are actually used to describe the character (for example, *brave, hard-hearted, wise, curious, irresponsible*). Adjectives often signal key character traits.

To get started writing a character sketch, you might want to organize your notes in a T-chart. Here is a sample chart based on the narrator from Edgar Allan Poe's short story "The Tell-Tale Heart":

Adjective, characteristic, or character trait	Specific example or quotation
obsessed	• is haunted by the old man's eye; wants to kill him because of this
patient	• doesn't rush to murder; instead, waits a long time after old man wakes up suddenly
organized	• well-prepared: plans to hide body under floorboards; tub to catch blood
guilty	• conscience gives him away when police question him

Written out in full, the notes on the previous page might result in the following character sketch:

Sample Character Sketch

The narrator of Edgar Allan Poe's "The Tell-Tale Heart" is an unusual character to say the least. What first catches the reader's attention is how obsessed the narrator is with the old man's "vulture" eye: "Whenever it fell upon me, my blood ran cold." The narrator is actually very patient. He takes a week to kill his victim, even waiting more than an hour to complete the deed.

The narrator also reveals himself to be arrogant and organized. He is very methodical in the way he disposes of the body, and brags: "There was nothing to wash out—no stain of any kind—no blood-spot whatever." His guilty conscience finally catches up with him, however. At first, he is very controlled and friendly with the police. Eventually, though, because of his conscience, he begins to imagine hearing the beating of the old man's heart and he confesses his deed. There is no doubt that this guilt still haunts him and that he really is insane and not just "nervous," as he claims to be at the beginning of the story.

Profile

A profile is a brief biography of a person. It usually provides a description of the individual's unique career and life, as well as insights into his or her feelings, thoughts, and social environment.

Tips for Writing a Profile

People are interested in the lives of other people, which means that well-written profiles are very popular with readers. Here are some tips to help you create a successful profile.

- Pick someone you think will interest a fairly wide audience. This person could be someone you know, such as a member of your family or community, or someone who is widely recognized and considered a newsworthy public personality.

- Once you have decided on your subject, think about your purpose for writing the profile. What do you want to show about the person? Why is he or she worthy of a profile?

- Profiles are usually arranged chronologically (in order of time), though some might start with the person's current achievement, then go back into the past to trace the road to success. Profiles often tell about important life stages such as early childhood, school years, family life, and early work experiences.

- Pay close attention to transitions between the different life stages. Be specific in identifying these changes in place or time (for example, *Three years later, Dennis met Raisa when he moved to California to explore the film industry*).

- Be sure your facts are accurate. At the same time, look for details that are unique or are likely to grab your audience's attention. Given the preceding example, if a teacher had predicted that Dennis would be famous someday, that's the kind of comment worth noting.

- As you would do in a character sketch, include details and events that you think give insight into your subject's personality and character. For example, if you want to communicate that an actor likes performing in movies but not on stage, you might describe an incident from the actor's childhood in which he or she had a bad case of stage fright.

- When describing the person's character, use descriptive adjectives such as *vain, unselfish, practical, generous, ambitious,* and *determined.* Support whatever adjectives you choose with examples.

- Include some direct statements made by the person to add authenticity. If you're interviewing the person, an audio recorder is normally acceptable (as long as the person has agreed to its use). Later, you can transcribe or pick notable quotes to use in your profile.

- If you're interviewing the person, be sure you've written down enough questions to ask. Call ahead to arrange and confirm your interview time. Be polite and thank the person at the end of the interview. Sending a thank-you card or note is also a common courtesy after an interview.

- Talk to people who know your subject either directly or through reading or research they've done. They will provide useful information and a range of views to help you create a well-rounded profile.

Think about how these tips apply to the following sample profile.

Sample Profile

Sidney Crosby: NHL Phenomenon

I'm more concerned about meeting my own expectations,

not the ones other people set for me.

Sidney Crosby—otherwise known as Sid the Kid, the Next Gretzky, Baby Legs, and The Pride of Cole Harbour—probably knows himself better than anyone else. Some have described him as the saviour of the NHL and the face of the league. This is high praise for a young player who at 18 was drafted first by the Pittsburgh Penguins and mentored in his rookie year by the legendary Mario Lemieux.

But #87 has long had to live with the opinions of others. In fact, it was

Wayne Gretzky, the long-time superstar, who himself predicted that Crosby might match or better Gretzky's records. Talk about pressure for a young hockey star born in Halifax on August 7, 1987!

Crosby's childhood was not unlike that of many other kids who grew up playing Nintendo, watching cartoons such as *Teenage Mutant Ninja Turtles*, and imitating Bret Hart wrestling moves. His bedroom walls were decorated with Montréal Canadiens wallpaper and Gretzky and Lemieux posters.

Like Gretzky, Crosby got started young, shooting pucks at the family clothes dryer in the basement and getting on the ice when he was just three. As with Gretzky, Crosby's father has probably been his most significant influence, helping the hockey prodigy develop his basic skills early on and teaching him to be a decent person who respects others.

Crosby's development can be measured by the fact that he played with 10-year-olds when he was 6 and 17-year-olds when he was 14. That's not your average player. In those early years, the highly productive forward got 280 points playing at the Atom level in 1997 and 162 points in 57 games during his grade 10 year with a high school in Minnesota. In two seasons with Rimouski Oceanic, he accumulated an astounding plus-minus rating of +127!

In his teens, Crosby was mentored by Andy O'Brien, later a training coach for the Florida Panthers. O'Brien set up a five-year advanced conditioning program, which involved doing sprints while wearing weights. Crosby was a fast learner, and he now has an incredibly strong torso that is durable and balanced. This makes him very tough to knock down.

Crosby's agile body also gives him a fast-moving stride. He has "soft hands" (skilful puck-handling ability), a quick shot, and a great pass. In fact, his teammates always have to be on the alert for what seem like impossible passes. Crosby, you see, has excellent "vision" and can predict plays before they happen, his intense stare envisioning what other, more ordinary, hockey players cannot.

All this has helped him become the youngest player to score 100 points in one season and 200 career points (done in two seasons). In 2007, just his second year with the Penguins, he scored a hat trick of NHL trophies: the Hart Memorial Trophy, the Art Ross Trophy, and the Lester B. Pearson Trophy. The team subsequently made him the youngest captain in the NHL, and the big commercial endorsements naturally followed—with Reebok, Telus, and Pepsi.

And how has all this affected Canada's latest hockey phenomenon? Has it changed his character? Not much. Crosby remains humble and admits no one is likely to match Gretzky's records. Conscious of his role-model status, he continues to sign autographs for his young fans, who regard him as something of a teen idol. But he is self-confident, too, and handles himself well with the media, who have been critical of him since he entered the NHL.

No one questions Crosby's toughness and will. He played with a broken foot, without complaining, in the 2007 playoff series with Ottawa. His natural talent is also unquestionable. He was just 16 when he scored a goal for Team Canada in the 2003 Junior World Championships, the youngest player on record to do so. He has always been a great leader and elevates the game of those around him.

And what accomplishments are next for Sid the Kid? According to Crosby, "I'm still learning and still going to make mistakes, but I'm ready for the challenge."

Book Review

A book review consists of a reader's opinions on specific aspects of a fiction or non-fiction book. The review describes and evaluates the book, as well as its meaning and significance.

What to Address in a Book Review

When writing a book review, try to provide information about, and then comment on, the following:

- the author's purpose for writing the book
- the audience for whom it seems to be written (for example, a wide readership or a specific audience, such as teenagers or hockey fans)
- relevant author information (for example, anything that relates to the content of the book review, such as the author's qualifications or major influences)
- the genre (type) of book (for example, biography, history, essay collection, fantasy novel, mystery novel, or self-help book)
- the theme and main ideas
- the book's organization
- the author's style (for example, use of language and devices such as flashback)
- the relationship of the book to other works by the same author
- the relationship of the book to other similar books about the same topic or of the same genre
- the book's strengths and weaknesses

Tips for Writing a Book Review

Here are some general tips for writing any book review, no matter the genre or type of book. Immediately following this list are specific tips for reviewing fiction and non-fiction.

- Read the book with an open mind, giving it a chance to speak for itself. Do not decide beforehand that you will or will not like the book for reasons such as what's on its cover or what you've heard others say about it.

- Reread more difficult parts as necessary.

- Make notes as you read or reread, collecting quotations and other details to which you may want to refer in your review.

- Decide whether you generally like, dislike, or have a mixed opinion about the book. This will help to focus your comments. Word the title of your review to reflect your opinion.

- After your title, at the top of your review, record the following:
  – book title

  – author name(s)

  – publisher

  – place of publication and copyright date

  – number of pages

- Near the beginning of your review, give a brief overview or summary of the plot or ideas presented in the book. However, don't make this the main focus of your review.

- Use short, key quotations from the book to support your views or to clarify the book's content.

- How did the book affect you? What did you like or dislike most about it?

- Would you recommend the book to other readers? Why or why not? What kind of audience would be most interested in reading it?

- Finally, keep your own readers in mind by making your writing lively and informative.

Questions to Help You Review Fiction

- Are the plot and characters believable and realistic? If the book is a fantasy, are the plot and characters impressively imaginative?

- Are setting and atmosphere effectively used?

- From whose point of view is the story told? Does this point of view work effectively?

- Are the theme and how it's handled familiar or original? Does the theme have broad significance?

- How well does the author handle dialogue, description, and stylistic devices such as imagery and foreshadowing?

Questions to Help You Review Non-fiction

- What are the author's qualifications and background for writing on this topic? Is the author objective or biassed?

- Is the author's account of the person, events, or topic adequate and sufficiently complete?

- Is the information familiar, or new and original?

- What are the author's views about the person, events, or topic? How convincing and accurate is the author's presentation of facts and details?

- How accurate and reliable are the author's sources?

- How well are visual materials such as photographs, charts, and maps used?

Sample Book Review

Crabbe: a great adventure story, even if too unrealistic

Crabbe by William Bell, Toronto: Fitzhenry & Whiteside, 2006, 192 pages

"I was sick of my life and already sick of the future that everybody had planned for me, but nobody bothered to consult me about" (20).

How many young adults have either spoken or thought those words? I know I have. I think I'm considered by most to be a normal, well-adjusted kind of person. I do argue occasionally with my parents and siblings, I do question my teachers, and I do think that much of what I see happening around me is hypocritical and therefore wrong. So I don't have a problem with Franklin Crabbe, the protagonist of the novel *Crabbe*, and the questions for which he needs to find answers. How he goes about finding those answers, however, is something else.

The plot of the novel is fairly straightforward, a story about a kid in grade 12 on the eve of his final exams. An otherwise normal 18-year-old, he feels that he's been badly treated, so he decides to run away from home—far away from home. Though he's supposedly bright, he's very naive about, and totally unprepared for, the path he's chosen for himself. He is saved from death and befriended by a capable but lonely and mysterious backwoods mentor named Mary. Over time, the two come to share many things: adventures, freedoms, secrets, and survival.

The novel is presented as a first-person diary and is carefully structured. Except for the book's opening and closing chapters, it is told through a long flashback. This organization works well, because it allows the narrator to "grow" in both his own and the reader's eyes. The story opens with the narrator in a psychiatric ward playing "word-chess" with a doctor. The discussion between the two introduces some of the themes that run through the book: adult/teen conflict, family dysfunction, the need for freedom, and rebellion. By the end of the story, the reader can add the themes of friendship, identity, and self-discovery to this list.

What comes through most strongly is a story of a very anxious teenager. Many of the adults in the story are awful people—very strict parents, authoritarian teachers, a controlling doctor, and villainous hunters. Other adults, however, are presented more positively—his mentor, his English teacher, and an old nurse. Is this a realistic balance of good and evil? Perhaps. It certainly does show the reader the extremes of both. That's my main criticism of the book: that it goes to extremes to get across its points. There's great action, including a near-drowning, a bear attack, a snowstorm, an attempted murder, and an amputation. I wonder, though, if all that—along with the many negative, stereotyped characterizations such as those of the parents and the doctor—is just too much, too unrealistic? Readers will need to decide for themselves.

At the conclusion of the novel, and even more as I sit back to think longer about it, I find myself frustrated by how the author "sells out" his protagonist with the ending. While Bell himself has said, "I wanted to write a story around the idea of taking control of one's life" (www.schoolinfo.ca/read/authors/bell/bellQuestions.htm), his resolution seems to me to be a cop-out. Perhaps his being in his mid-40s when he wrote it has something to do with this. Nonetheless, the book is definitely worth the read. It gives the reader lots to think about and to discuss.

Is it a book for guys? Will girls enjoy it as well? Both, I think. It's a great adventure story with lots of action. It also shows a broad range of emotions. At the same time, though, the reader gets to consider the questions a "misfit" must resolve as he attempts to make sense of his life.

Movie Review

A movie review is essentially a decision-making tool for anyone thinking of going to see a particular movie. The review must therefore be informed and fair, providing the reader with a description of the movie and an evaluation of its strengths and weaknesses.

What to Address in a Movie Review

When writing a movie review, try to provide information about, and then comment on, the following:

- the movie's intended audience

- the director, mentioning previous films this person has directed (if you know any)

- the genre (type) of movie (for example, action, horror, science fiction, romance, or comedy)

- the plot and the theme(s) it addresses

- details about who is starring in the movie, and how well they acted

- the key scenes in the movie, noting their importance to the story as a whole

- your views on one or more of the movie's special effects (if any), its use of music, and the quality of the camera work

- your overall opinion or evaluation to help the reader decide whether the movie might be worth seeing

Tips for Writing a Movie Review

- Take notes while you watch the movie to ensure you don't forget any important details (and your thoughts about them).

- Determine your audience. Are you writing for people your own age and with the same interests, or for a wider audience?

- Formulate your opinion about the movie in one sentence. This can serve as the main idea that focusses your review.

- Outline for your own reference the plot of the movie, and briefly describe the opening scene, identifying any questions the movie seems to be asking in those first few minutes.

- Most of your review should focus on the movie's plot and the quality of its acting. Evaluate the effectiveness of the plot and discuss important scenes that reveal character. Analyse the characters, their dialogue, and how they interact with one another.

- Don't spoil your readers' enjoyment of the film by telling them too much of the plot. Be careful not to give away the ending or any surprise plot twists.

- Explain why you liked or disliked the movie. If you describe the plot as unconvincing, explain in what ways it is unconvincing. If you say the dialogue is powerful, provide an example.

- Do not unfairly compare this movie with others of a different genre. For example, you can't expect a love story to have thrilling action sequences or special effects.

- Be honest in your opinions, but be fair. If the movie has both strong and weak points, mention both, giving credit where it's due. Disliking a movie doesn't license you to write a nasty review.

- Create a memorable title for your review, one that indicates to your reader whether you think the film is worth seeing or not.

- Write with enthusiasm! Even if you don't like a particular film, chances are you are a fan of movies and this should come through in your writing.

Sample Movie Review

Into the Wild: a memorable journey

Many young people think about running away from home at some point in their lives. Few do so, however. Those who try it usually don't go far and don't stay away for long. The central character of *Into the Wild* does just the opposite.

Director and screenwriter Sean Penn's film is an excellent adaptation of Jon Krakauer's bestseller of the same name. Christopher McCandless (Emile Hirsch) is an idealistic young man who hitchhikes to Alaska to live in the wild. Penn's movie is true to the plot, characters, locales, and spirit of the original book, so readers of the book will not be disappointed. All told, the movie is a sensitive and realistic portrayal of character defects that lead to an unusual and unnecessary tragedy.

McCandless is a puzzle. It's not clear why he abandons his family in the first place. He and his sister Carine (Jena Malone), the poetic narrator of much of the story, seem too connected for him not to tell her where he has gone. Although McCandless is a college graduate, his acts of defiance against his parents' ambitions for him seem very adolescent, such as when he burns the last of his money. At one point, Carine herself reflects, "Something more than rebellion … was driving him." It drives him, in fact, to crisscross the United States before finally arriving at his dream of a "great Alaskan adventure."

It seems strange at times that McCandless wants to be alone so much, since he is so naturally sociable. He charms everyone he meets—the man who offers him both work and friendship, the aging hippie couple who also appear to be searching for something beyond themselves, the young girl with a crush on him, the war vet whose tears tell how deeply he feels. They all seem to sense that McCandless needs to be protected from something—but from what?

He certainly doesn't need to be protected from himself; he proves himself very capable in many areas. He is able to get into Harvard, bury his identity, drive a combine, run the Colorado River rapids in a kayak, and even sweet-talk a border guard. He also has great strength of spirit. The viewer is allowed to glimpse "the core of man's spirit [that] comes from new experiences."

McCandless's big dreams are powerfully conveyed on screen. Split-screen images, some slow-motion movement, and contrasts of light and dark all heighten the viewer's experience of what McCandless is experiencing.

Sean Penn has directed a fine movie, richly supported by original music from Eddie Vedder of Pearl Jam. Penn's handling of flashbacks and reflective voice-overs are well placed, and accomplished performers, such as Hal Holbrook as McCandless's surrogate father, ably assist him.

The film raises questions but only hints at possible answers. The mystery, though, is not so much "What happened?" which might be the easier puzzle to resolve, but "Who was he?" As a viewer, you'll leave the theatre wondering, but you'll be moved by a character who miscalculated the challenge of surviving once he went "into the wild."

News Report

A news report informs newspaper readers about a particular event or issue of current interest. Typically, the report deals with something that has happened very recently (such as a natural disaster) or the latest developments in an ongoing project (such as the addition of more bike lanes to community streets).

There are three key characteristics of good news writing: accurate information, clear statements, and a reader-friendly style.

- Accurate information consists of the correct details related to the events or issues being reported. These details include the sequence of events, causes and location, names of people involved, and things said at the scene. These details should reflect what occurred or what's involved in an issue.

- Clear statements conveying this information are essential. The diction in the report should be specific and precise (for example, rather than *late last night*, say *at 10:15 last night during a thunderstorm*). Short, closely connected sentences also help readers to follow what's being reported.

- A reader-friendly style includes vivid descriptions of an event and memorable quotations from individuals involved in the story. The style also highlights the most interesting aspects of an issue.

The two most common types of news reports are hard news stories and feature stories.

Hard News Stories

Look at the front page of any daily newspaper. What you see are hard news stories, which communicate information on current events. Preceding all hard news stories is a headline, often accompanied by a photograph. Both are meant to hook the reader. Such stories answer the basic questions of journalism: the 5Ws + H.

What happened?	**W**here did it happen?
Who was involved?	**W**hen did it happen?
Why did it happen?	**H**ow did it happen?

Writers of hard news stories assume that their readers are in a hurry. They therefore provide as much key information up front as possible. This allows the newspaper reader with only a few minutes to spare to quickly pick up the essential facts of the story—the headline plus the *what, where, who,* and *when.* For the

reader with more time, the *why* and *how* can be found later in the report. This structure is referred to as an inverted pyramid.

As you would expect, a hard news story is always written in the past tense in an objective way, using the third person. This means presenting just the facts without expressing your own views, as you would in more subjective writing, such as an opinion piece. (See Point of View, page 76.)

I keep six honest serving-men
(They taught me all I knew);
Their names are What and
Why and When
And How and Where and
Who.

Rudyard Kipling

The key to any effective news story is the lead (the opening sentence or two of the story). The purpose of the lead is to summarize the story and to engage the reader immediately. Although it is brief, the lead provides answers to at least the first four of the 5Ws questions. The lead that follows comes from a community newspaper.

> Dozens of concerned students rallied in front of the school board office at midday yesterday. They were protesting the federal government's most recent declaration on the Kyoto Accord.

The body of the news story supports the headline and the lead by including such details as additional facts and statements made by people involved in the story. This helps to create a coherent and appealing narrative. The body

- expands on the information in the headline and lead
- addresses the questions of *what* (if more information is required), *why*, and *how*
- includes opinions expressed during or about the event, including direct quotations
- provides descriptive details
- sometimes adds information explaining any accompanying photographs

Feature Stories

Feature stories are news reports that are not as time-sensitive as hard news stories. They are written for readers who usually take the time to read a piece from beginning to end. Such stories emphasize background information, such as historical facts about a community initiative or profiles of individuals or organizations.

Feature stories

- focus on the *who, why,* and *how* of the event or issue rather than on the *what, where,* and *when*
- open with a paragraph that presents more than just the facts of a hard news story lead (for example, a short, personal account, or an attention-getting statement such as *Residents of Mapleville are so fed up with their local councillors that they plan to kick them out of office before the month is over*)
- make greater use of direct quotations from newsmakers, which often result from conducting actual interviews with them
- incorporate some background research
- include some of the writer's first-person impressions, but, as with a hard news story, do not include any direct expression of personal opinions or judgments about the issue or event

Notice how these characteristics are reflected in the following sample feature story.

Timberlea teen helps, two shoes at a time

By Joel Jacobson

The door to Sacred Heart Catholic Church Hall in Timberlea bursts open for the umpteenth time. In walks Michael Murphy in sock feet and holding a pair of shoes in his hand. "Here, Matthew. Here are more shoes for your project," he laughs.

Michael's nephew, Matthew Burke, has been collecting shoes, sneakers, and boots for three weeks, footwear that will make winter more comfortable for a group of men who call Metro Turning Point their temporary home.

While Michael's shoes weren't included, two pairs of boots, one new and one used, that his daughter Kathleen brought certainly were.

"We saw your story on television and had to help out," Kathleen says with pride to her cousin.

Today, Matthew is collecting at the hall. Television and other promotions have drawn men, women, and children from the community, and their mostly new footwear, to this unique drive, called Shoes for the Shelter.

Matthew is 14, a grade 9 student at Ridgcliffe Middle School in Beechville. A few weeks ago, the youngster from Timberlea Village saw a story in *The Chronicle Herald* about the executive director of Metro Turning Point, Michael Poworoznyk, experiencing two days as a homeless man, living on the streets as the men he assists and oversees do.

"I had no idea what these men go through until I read that article," Matt says. "Then I realized how they have to walk from Turning Point to somewhere else for breakfast and then to lunch, and dinner, and to the shelter again."

He visited the centre with his mother, Karen, a member of Turning Point's board of directors.

"We went to the shelter and saw piles of shoes—golf shoes, women's shoes, old sneakers. The men were taking whatever they could use to walk on the streets," Karen says. "Matthew was very moved by what he saw and decided he'd try to find as many pairs of men's shoes as he could."

Last week, Matthew, his mother, his father, Norm, and his eight-year-old brother, Patrick, delivered to the shelter 250 pairs of shoes, sneakers, and boots, $700 in cash, two moving-size boxes of socks, one box of toiletries, three of winter clothing, and one of other clothing. Matthew was overwhelmed.

"I know how tough it is for the homeless men to acquire shoes, and for Metro Turning Point to find shoes for them. Footwear is so expensive. And when these men have improper footwear, they can get fungus and blisters and that can be very uncomfortable."

Matthew, an honour roll and French immersion student, a member of First Timberlea Scout Troop, active in community basketball with the St. Margaret's Bay Slam, and involved in religious education programs at Sacred Heart, is also a well-organized young man.

In mid-November, on his own, he prepared a flyer to place at the church and school. He appeared on television. And the shoes started to accumulate.

"My focus was awareness," he says. "The need is there. It wasn't hard to organize this and it will certainly greatly benefit these men."

Karen says men at the shelter are usually last on the list of those needing help.

"Most people think of women and children at other shelters, which is wonderful, but these men need help, too. Matthew has kept a log of hours he'd given to this and he's over 30 in the last three to four weeks. He realized 10 percent of people take action while 90 percent think it should be done. We're so proud he's among the 10 percent."

On this collection day, Matthew doesn't slow down. He lets others talk while he accepts footwear and other items from generous donors, counts and packs them, and continues with his goal of helping men in need.

Summary

A summary is a shortened version of a speech, news report, magazine article, profile, or section of a textbook that you write in your own words. In a summary, you show that you understand the original piece by highlighting its main idea and most important points.

Steps for Writing a Summary

1. Read the source carefully once or twice to develop a general understanding of its theme or message. If the source is a news report, take note of its headline. If the source is an article or section of a textbook, take note of its title and any subheadings. These will help you identify quickly what content is in the source.

2. Identify the thesis statement in the source, if applicable. In some cases, this appears as the first or last sentence in the first paragraph. Write down this sentence word for word on a separate sheet of paper. Next, read this sentence again to make sure you understand what it's saying. Then rewrite it in your own words.

   If your source is a newspaper or magazine article that begins with an anecdote (short, personal account) or other hook to pull you into the story, ask yourself, "What idea is this writer's beginning trying to get across to me?" Write your answer on a separate sheet of paper.

3. Identify the topic sentences or main points in the source, ignoring supporting details such as examples or quotations. Write these points on your sheet of paper in your own words and in the order in which they appear in the source. Along with what you've written in Step 2, you now have a draft of your summary.

4. Reread the source to make sure your draft summary accurately reflects the original.

5. Revise your draft, if necessary, and then write a final copy of your summary. The final copy should:
   • be written in your own words

- reflect only what's in the original source, with no thoughts of your own included
- be significantly shorter than the original by about 80 to 90 percent

What follows is a summary of the feature story that begins on page 109.

Sample Summary

"Timberlea teen helps, two shoes at a time" by Joel Jacobson

This feature news story is about grade 9 student Matthew Burke trying to find footwear for homeless men at the Metro Turning Point men's shelter in Halifax. An active and able student in Beechville, Nova Scotia, Matthew learned of the need for winter clothing from a news story about Metro Turning Point, which he then visited. He was so affected by what he saw that he took action. He decided to focus on men's shoes and try to raise public awareness of the homeless. The article lists the many hours invested, and the results: donations of all kinds, not just footwear.

Opinion Piece

In an opinion piece, a writer expresses his or her point of view on an issue. The writer does so mainly to help readers understand that view, and sometimes to try to get them to agree with it. Opinion pieces are commonly featured in newspapers and magazines, where they appear as editorials and op-ed pieces (which are published on the page **op**posite the **ed**itorial page). In school, opinion pieces are often given as assignments.

Opinion writers typically present an answer to a question that concerns the wider community (for example, *Should 16-year-olds be permitted to vote in local, provincial, or federal elections?*). People have different views on questions like this, and writing an opinion piece is one way to share how strongly you feel about an issue.

Opinion pieces vary in length, depending on how much the writer has to say and how many words are allowed for the assignment. Whatever the length, if the opinion piece is to be persuasive it must have a strong beginning, middle, and end.

The Beginning

The introductory paragraph of an opinion piece introduces the issue by stating why it's of public concern and relevant to the writer's audience. This beginning should also indicate why the writer is interested in the particular issue, and state clearly which side of the issue she or he supports. The writer's statement of position becomes the article's thesis statement. Here is a possible opening paragraph for an opinion piece on the voting age.

Before the last federal election, teenagers 16 years of age, like me, campaigned across the country for the right to vote. Unfortunately, we did not get our wish. Many people heard us, however, perhaps for the first time. I believe that if we continue to campaign, people will not only hear but also listen. That's when 16-year-olds will finally get a right that should have been theirs a long time ago.

The Middle (Body)

The middle, or body, of the opinion piece presents the details that support the writer's opinion. The details must be both relevant—that is, they must relate directly to the issue—and specific. Broad statements are not enough to persuade an audience.

Details might consist of

- the writer's own reasons for taking a particular stance and why these reasons are valid

- facts that relate directly to the issue

- specific anecdotes or examples from the writer's own involvement with the issue (or the involvement of others)

- suggestions or illustrations of what's likely to happen if one side or the other is accepted

- descriptions of issue-related situations that readers can readily understand

Some writers begin the body of their opinion piece with a short summary of both sides of the issue. Others prefer to address both sides of the issue throughout the piece, showing why one side of an argument is better than the other. End your discussion of each point with a statement of why you think that point should be accepted or rejected. Note how this is done in the following paragraph, which highlights different examples of responsible behaviour by 16-year-olds.

Tips for Writing Opinion Pieces

- Stay focussed on the issue. Try not to get sidetracked by a related, but different, issue.

- Some expressions, such as "I believe that … " are acceptable when they are used for emphasis. However, use *I* sparingly. Using *I* too often can make your piece seem too personal and biassed.

Adults may say that 16-year-olds are not responsible enough to vote, but they need to look at how the world has changed, and how teenagers have changed along with it. Many of us already handle adult responsibilities. More teenagers than not hold down part-time jobs on top of their daily duties as students. Along with our jobs, we pay income taxes to help society function. Most of us also show responsibility by holding driver's licences, owning cars, and paying for gas and insurance. As well, many teens give their time generously in volunteer work. I myself volunteer in a nursing home, as do several of my friends, and the residents of the home seem more than happy to treat us as adult friends. So, if we already contribute in these ways to society, why should we not be allowed to contribute further with our collective voices at election time?

In the body paragraphs of an opinion piece, you should aim to present enough well-supported points to support your opinion on the issue.

The End

Opinion pieces typically conclude with a relatively short paragraph that summarizes the writer's point of view. In some ways the closing paragraph restates the thesis of the opinion piece, though in different words. Often it will offer a suggestion as to how the issue can be resolved to everyone's satisfaction and benefit.

What makes a good citizen? Answers may vary, depending on whether you think ideal citizens are people who should mind their own business without making any noise, or people who are prepared to get involved on behalf of what they believe. Nonetheless, I think we can all agree that teenagers have much to offer. All we ask for is the opportunity to do so in the voting booth.

Research Paper

A research paper gives you the opportunity to investigate a topic thoroughly, and to present your findings with supporting documentation such as lists of sources. Writing a research paper involves the same stages of the writing process as writing an essay does: Understanding the Topic, Understanding Audience and Purpose, Brainstorming, Focussing on a Thesis, Collecting and Reviewing Information, Organizing Information, Writing a Draft, Revising, Editing, Proofreading, and Publishing a Final Copy.

A research paper differs from an essay, however, in the quantity and range of information that you're expected to collect, review, organize, and document. You must therefore plan very carefully, allowing yourself sufficient time to consider your topic, to identify and make use of relevant sources of information, and to create and present your paper.

Getting Started

Here are some tips for getting started with your research:

- Start early! Allow yourself enough time to do your research and write your paper, keeping in mind any other assignments you are required to complete.

- If you are selecting your own topic, check on the availability of information and resources first before committing to the topic. If the information is unavailable or insufficient, think of an alternative topic and check on what research material you can find for it.

- Consult with a librarian or library assistant. These specialists will help you locate key resources such as websites, magazines, reference books, and audiovisual materials.

Two other very useful ways to get your research underway are checking library catalogues and using Internet search engines.

Library Catalogues

Every library has a catalogue (usually accessed by computer) that lists print and electronic resources available in the library. Each resource is usually listed under at least three headings:

author, title, and subject. In computer files, you may also be able to search by content, key words, or in other ways. The main menu of the catalogue will list the choices available to you.

Periodical Indexes

Most libraries or learning resource centres also stock the *Readers' Guide to Periodical Literature* and the *Canadian Periodical Index.* These are excellent basic resources for identifying up-to-date print articles in more than 300 magazines such as *Discover, Maclean's, National Geographic, Newsweek, Reader's Digest,* and *Time.* Both indexes list articles by subject and author.

Internet Search Engines

The Internet offers a number of search engines that can help you quickly identify sources of information for your topic. Popular search engines include AltaVista, Google, and Yahoo!

Keep the following in mind when you use a search engine:

- As with library catalogues, start by entering a key word or phrase, and make sure to put quotation marks around any phrase you use. This way, the search engine will identify all sites containing that exact phrase. Otherwise, the resulting hits from the search will include all web pages that contain any of the words in the phrase. It's also a good idea to have a list of alternative words and phrases to try in case your first search is unsuccessful.

- If you find the list of websites is too long, try eliminating those posted by individuals or businesses. Educational or government sites tend to be more objective and balanced. You can easily identify such sites by the last letters in their addresses, or URLs (Uniform Resource Locators).

Educational site	*.edu* or *.ac*
International organization site	*.int*
Canadian federal government site	*.gc.ca*
Not-for-profit organization site	*.org*
Government site (usually American)	*.gov*

Sources of Research Information

Often, you'll find the research information you're looking for in these sources:

- print and non-print materials such as histories, biographies, dictionaries, almanacs, magazine and newspaper articles and reviews, maps, reference books, atlases, videos, and CD-ROMs

- recordings from broadcast media, such as television and radio

- interviews and surveys

Encyclopedias

Libraries typically carry encyclopedias, which provide basic information about a subject or person. Some popular encyclopedias include *The Canadian Encyclopedia, Encyclopedia Britannica, World Book Encyclopedia, Collier's Encyclopedia, Current Biography, McGraw-Hill Yearbook of Science and Technology, The World Almanac and Book of Facts, Who's Who*, and *Encyclopedia of World Biography*. Many encyclopedias are also available for use online, free of charge.

Entries in encyclopedias tend to be brief and offer only general information, but they frequently include suggestions for other related topics and resources.

As well, there are specialized encyclopedias such as *Benet's Reader's Encyclopedia* and *Halliwell's Filmgoer's Companion*. The former provides specialized information pertaining to literature, while the latter focusses on the film industry.

Websites

Through sites on the World Wide Web, you can discover more information about your research topic. These sources are usually more up-to-date than books or periodicals, but you should approach them with caution. Anyone, including individuals and businesses promoting a cause or looking to make money, can post information on a website. As a result, what you read and view on a site may be inaccurate or biassed, that is, slanted in some way to promote particular views or interests. You should check all facts you find on a website against at least two other sources.

Useful websites, and the kind of information they offer, include the examples below. To find them, just enter their names in the search engine of your choice.

- Atlapedia: maps, facts, and statistics
- Bartlett's Familiar Quotations: quotations from a wide range of sources
- Biographical Dictionary: over 30,000 biographies of men and women from the present and past
- Canadian Encyclopedia: comprehensive reference work
- Columbia Encyclopedia: comprehensive reference work
- eHow: general information and how-to instructions arranged by category
- Encyclopedia.com: links to a wide range of on-line encyclopedias
- Google Accessible: search engine designed for people with visual disabilities
- HowStuffWorks: explanations of how things work, arranged by category
- Internet Movie Database: information about movies, television shows, actors, production crews, and video games

- Internet Public Library: on-line public library with links to government, educational, newspaper, and reference sites around the world

- Library of Congress Research Tools: links to on-line databases and other Internet resources, sponsored and maintained by the world's largest library

- MSN Encarta: encyclopedia articles, maps, a dictionary, a thesaurus, and more

- refdesk.com: links to a wide range of on-line sources such as newspapers, magazines, writing guides, and atlases

- Rotten Tomatoes: movie reviews, previews, trailers, and general information

- suite101.com: interactive on-line magazine with articles categorized by area, such as history, music, technology, sports, and health and wellness

CD-ROMs

Portable databases for publications such as *National Geographic* and for some encyclopedias and reference books are available on CD-ROM. Check to see what's available in your school's library or learning resource centre.

Interviews

Interviews are a good way to get expert opinions. The first-hand information given in an interview can make your topic come alive for your reader. Here are some tips to consider when handling interviews:

- Decide how you will conduct the interview: by phone, by mail/e-mail, or in person. Unless the person you're interviewing (the interviewee) is a close friend or relative, never meet anyone alone. Choose a public place, and bring someone with you. Tell a parent or guardian where you are going.

- Arrive prepared by first doing some background research on the topic. You will be able to ask more specific questions if you know your topic well.

- Formulate questions that only the interviewee can answer. Word your questions so that they cannot be answered with a simple *yes* or *no* (for example, ask *how* and *why* questions).

- Take notes, or use an audio recorder (with the interviewee's permission) for direct quotations. Immediately after the interview, read over your notes, clarify any scribbles or abbreviations, and jot down remembered ideas.

- Very soon after the interview, send a card, letter, or e-mail thanking the interviewee.

Evaluating the Usefulness of Sources

You want information from sources to be as useful and relevant as possible. Use the following checklist to help you evaluate what you've found.

✓ Will the source be of interest to your audience?

✓ Is the information relevant to your topic?

✓ Is the information up to date?

✓ Is the source sufficiently complete, with supporting details provided?

✓ Is the author or interviewee providing the information an authority on the topic? What are her or his credentials?

✓ To what extent is the information objective and balanced? To what extent is it influenced by the author's or interviewee's point of view on particular issues? (Be especially careful with websites in this regard.)

✓ Is the source identified as useful and cross-referenced in other reliable sources?

Initial Documenting of Sources

Once you've identified the sources you intend to use for your research paper, you need to start documenting, or noting down, basic information about them for use in footnotes, endnotes, and lists of sources. Document the following seven kinds of information for each source:

- call numbers (located on the spine) for any library material

- title

- author, editors, or other creators of information

- publisher

- publication date
- place of publication or URL
- date of interview, if applicable

Quotations and Citations

During the research stage, copy direct quotations onto small cards (or separate pages, one per print source consulted), along with the documentation details of the source. With the quotations documented separately, you can easily reorder them and eliminate at a later date those you don't want to use.

Inserting Longer Quotations

Longer quotations (block quotations) are separated from the body of the research paper and indented from the left margin. No quotation marks are needed because the indenting signals that it is quoted material. You can edit a longer quotation (more than four lines) by substituting ellipsis points (three spaced periods) within square brackets for words that are left out. The example that follows is based on the feature story that begins on page 109.

According to Matthew's mother, Karen, homeless men at the shelter are often among the last to receive help. She adds:

> Most people think of women and children at other shelters, which is wonderful, but these men need help, too. Matthew [...] realized 10 percent of people take action while 90 percent think it should be done. We're so proud he's among the 10 percent. (Jacobsen C3)

Clearly, we all need to do more to help these forgotten citizens in our community.

Inserting Shorter Quotations

When you use a shorter quotation (fewer than four lines), it's best to embed it within a sentence, using opening and closing double quotation marks.

> According to Matthew's mother, Karen, "Most people think of women and children at other shelters, which is wonderful, but these men need help, too" (Jacobsen C3).

Citing Inserted Quotations

In the MLA (Modern Language Association) documentation style, which is used in the sample research paper beginning on page 128, sources for quotations are given in parentheses within the text.

Below is an example of one longer quotation and one shorter quotation using the MLA style. Note that it is enough to give the author's name and the page number of the quote if the entire source is included in the Works Cited list at the end of the research paper.

> In Robert Frost's "The Road Not Taken," the speaker is indecisive about what he wants to accomplish. As one critic points out: "When he starts out in life, he can't see that far into the future" (McKenzie 18). In the third stanza, the speaker discovers that it is impossible to go back in time once he has committed to one road or path through life:
>
> > He believed that he could come back another time
> > in the future, but as we all know this is impossible.
> > We can never return to the exact same point or
> > moment in the past. He is finally resolved to this
> > fact. (Shankar 17)
>
> The last stanza is about how taking one road determined his career and life....

Footnotes or Endnotes

Another option for documenting sources is using superscript (small raised) numbers at the end of each in-text reference. These numbers correspond to source information that is placed either at the bottom of the page (footnotes), or on a separate page at the end of the paper (endnotes), immediately before the Works Cited or Bibliography list.

If the corresponding footnote or endnote is the first documentation of a work, it includes complete source information (author name, source title, details of the publication, and the page number where the quotation can be found). Subsequent footnotes or endnotes for the same source are condensed versions of the first note.

Avoiding Plagiarism

You may choose to paraphrase a quotation, especially if it's very long. When you paraphrase, you're putting the original writer's ideas into your own words. Some people mistakenly believe that if they change the wording of a quotation, it is no longer quoted material and does not need to be acknowledged. That is incorrect. As long as the ideas belong to someone else, you still need to acknowledge the source even though you change the wording. Plagiarism (presenting the work of another as your own) is never acceptable.

Documenting Sources at the End of a Research Paper

At the end of your research paper, list on one or more separate pages all the sources actually cited in your text. In the MLA style, this list is titled Works Cited. The APA (American Psychological Association) style calls this list References, while *The Chicago Manual of Style* prefers the term Bibliography.

Whichever title is used, sources are arranged in this list alphabetically by authors' surnames. For each source listed in the MLA, APA, and Chicago styles, indent all lines except the first line.

Let's now take a closer look at each of the three main styles for Works Cited/References/Bibliographies. When you are writing a research paper, stick with one style, whether you are instructed by your teacher to use it or have chosen it yourself. Note carefully the sequence of the different parts of each item on the list, such as authors' and publishers' names, and how capitalization and punctuation are used.

MLA Style for Works Cited/Chicago Style for Bibliography

The MLA and Chicago styles for the following entries are the same, unless otherwise indicated.

A Book with One Author

Roussakis, Roula T. *Researching Your Family Tree.* Toronto: Donvale Press, 1998.

A Book with Two or More Authors

Eshpeter, James, and Harold Kotter. *Ways to Improve the Environment without Great Cost.* Toronto: Gage, 1998.

An Article or Chapter within a Source

MLA

Sexton, Deborah June. "Finding the Branches on Your Family Tree." *Family Tree Research.* Toronto: Webline Press, 1994. 88–90.

Chicago

Sexton, Deborah June. "Finding the Branches on Your Family Tree." In *Family Tree Research*, 88–90. Toronto: Webline Press, 1994.

A Newspaper or Magazine Article in Print

MLA

Strauss, Marina. "Retailers in the Grip of 'Tough' Times." *The Globe and Mail* 3 Jan. 2008: B1–2.

Chicago

Strauss, Marina. "Retailers in the Grip of 'Tough' Times." *The Globe and Mail,* January 3, 2008, B1–2.

A Newspaper or Magazine Article Online

MLA

Strauss, Marina. "Retailers in the Grip of 'Tough' Times." *The Globe and Mail* 3 Jan. 2008 <http://www.theglobeandmail.com/servlet/story/RTGAM.20080103.r-saan03/BNStory/Business>.

Chicago

Strauss, Marina. "Retailers in the Grip of 'Tough' Times." *The Globe and Mail* January 3, 2008. http://www.theglobeandmail.com/servlet/story/RTGAM.20080103.r-saan03/BNStory/Business.

A Website
MLA

The Purdue Online Writing Lab Home Page. English Department, Purdue University. 2 Jan. 2008 <http://owl.english.purdue.edu>.

Chicago

English Department, Purdue University. "The Purdue Online Writing Lab." http://owl.english.purdue.edu.

A Film
MLA

Ray. Dir. Taylor Hackford. Perf. Jamie Foxx, Kerry Washington, and Clifton Powell. Universal Pictures, 2004.

Chicago

Ray. Directed by Taylor Hackford. Universal Pictures, 2004.

A Television Program
MLA

"The Quality of Mercy." *Da Vinci's Inquest.* CBC. 28 Oct. 1998.

Chicago

Da Vinci's Inquest. "The Quality of Mercy," first broadcast 28 October 1998 by CBC. Directed by Stephen Surjik and written by Chris Haddock.

An Interview
MLA

Mungoshi, Dr. Epatha. Personal interview. 16 Apr. 2008.

Chicago

Chicago style allows only published or broadcast interviews to be listed in a bibliography, as follows:

Frum, Linda. "Peter Bergen Talks to Linda Frum." By Peter Bergen. *Maclean's,* January 30, 2006: 10–11.

An E-mail Message

Janvier, Frank. "Re: Research Project." E-mail to Emilia Chan. 17 Oct. 2007.

Chicago style does not require e-mails to be listed in a bibliography. Source information is usually given within the text or in a note.

APA Style for References

A Book with One Author
Roussakis, R. T. (1998). *Researching your family tree*. Toronto: Donvale Press.

A Book with Two or More Authors
Eshpeter, J., & H. Kotter. (1998). *Ways to improve the environment without great cost*. Toronto: Gage.

An Article or Chapter within a Source
Sexton, D. J. (1994). Finding the branches on your family tree. In *Family Tree Research*. (pp. 88–90). Toronto: Webline Press.

A Newspaper or Magazine Article in Print
Strauss, M. (2008, January 3). Retailers in the grip of 'tough' times. *The Globe and Mail*, B1–2.

A Newspaper or Magazine Article Online
Strauss, M. (2008). Retailers in the grip of 'tough' times. *The Globe and Mail*. B1–2. Retrieved January 3, 2008, from http://www.theglobeandmail.com/servlet/story/RTGAM.200 80103.r-saan03/BNStory/Business

A Website
English Department, Purdue University. (2008). The Purdue online writing lab. Retrieved January 2, 2008, from http://owl.english.purdue.edu

A Film
Hackford, T. (Producer & Director). (2004). *Ray* [Film]. United States: Universal Pictures.

A Television Program
Haddock, Chris (Writer), & Stephen Surjik (Director). October 28, 1998). The quality of mercy [Television series episode]. In *Da Vinci's Inquest*. Toronto: CBC.

A Published Interview
Frum, L. (2006, January 30). Peter Bergen talks to Linda Frum. *Maclean's*, 10–11.

The following sample research paper follows the MLA style for documentation.

Advertising's Effects on Teenagers

by Jackson Torres

English 9: Media Unit

Ms. Gupta

April 25, 2008

Advertising has a major effect on teenagers' values, health, lifestyles, and buying decisions. According to the Media Awareness Network, " … today's young people have become the most marketed-to generation in history, thanks to their spending power and their future clout as adult consumers" ("Marketing and Consumerism"). Businesses compete for the spending dollars of North American teenagers. This is because their personal spending totals $170 billion per year, or $101 a week per teen (Schor 23). Teenagers buy expensive items, such as designer clothes and electronic devices, but they also influence what their families buy. For instance, they recommend DVDs for home viewing and suggest fast-food restaurants for meals.

There is also a widespread view that teens are easy targets for brand loyalty, which can lead to long-term spending. A recent report by the Kaiser Family Foundation estimates that teens see an average of 40,000 ads a year just on television alone (Tamzarian). Teens are also targeted through magazines and movies, at sports events, in schools, and through various other media advertising, such as the kind found on the Internet.

Sadly, advertising's main message to teenagers is that they are inadequate or unacceptable. Ads take advantage of young people's insecurity and vulnerability. It's not surprising, then, that many ads focus on body image and attack self-esteem:

> A total of 69 percent of the girls [in a survey]
> reported that magazine pictures influenced their idea
> of the perfect body shape, and 47 percent reported
> wanting to lose weight because of magazine
> pictures. (Media Awareness Network 7)

Boys are similarly influenced to lose weight or pressured to develop muscle-bound bodies like those of many male athletes. Teens often associate "coolness" with a certain body type, which many ads promote as beautiful or sexually appealing. However, "it's important that young people understand that most of the images they see in the media are unrealistic and unattainable" (Media Awareness Network 7).

What's ironic is that advertising also plays upon young people's weakness for junk food. These ads push sugary soft drinks, salty and fatty snacks, and unhealthy fast foods such as hamburgers and pizza. Not surprisingly, teens and even very young children are facing what the Canadian Paediatric Society has described as an obesity epidemic. One in four Canadian children is considered overweight or obese (Tamzarian). Diabetes, respiratory problems, depression, and heart disease are all on the rise among young people.

Tobacco and alcohol ads also contribute to the adoption of risky habits and behaviours by too many teens. Even new tobacco products have been developed for particular markets. Camel No. 9 cigarettes, for example, are targeted to young women. Some social critics have speculated that ads forbidding smoking are actually increasing the number of smokers! It's also obvious that modern movies, much like older movies, have become the new advertising for smoking. "Eighty-two percent of youth-oriented PG-13 movies contain tobacco use" (Heyman 15). As consumer expert Juliet B. Schor comments: "The most important variable affecting smoking was the amount of time spent watching Hollywood movies" (135).

Alcohol ads bombard teenagers, especially teen males watching sports shows. It's impossible to watch any hockey game, for example, without seeing ads glorifying beer drinking as a fun activity. On an annual basis, teenagers see between 1,000 and 2,000 beer commercials carrying the message that "real" men drink beer ("Impact"). Recently, there has also been concern that young women are drinking more than they should. Advertisers spend millions of dollars targeting this new market with images of very young women in bars drinking fruit-flavoured liquors. In a recent series of articles about alcohol, Sharon Kirkey of *The Edmonton Journal* noted: "It takes less, usually, for women to get drunk because of their proportionately higher ratio of fat to water than men" (Kirkey A3).

There is no question that the power of advertising is changing teen health, values, and lifestyles. "Contemporary [North] American tweens and teens have emerged as the most brand-oriented, consumer-involved, and materialistic generations in history" (Schor 13). As an example, it's no longer enough for most teens to have just any clothing. Instead, many fashion-conscious teens are expected to wear the latest styles from brand names such as Adidas, Nike, Gap, Baby Phat, and American Eagle. One unspoken message communicated to teens appears to be this: if you can't afford to buy the latest "in" fashions, then you are a "loser" in yet a different way from the message about body image mentioned earlier.

It's clear that the pressure on teens to buy—and buy regularly—is relentless and dangerous. Perhaps the last word on this topic should go to a teenage consumer who is beginning to question the entire advertising process as it affects teenagers:

> I spend hundreds of dollars on make-up and
> products of every kind because I thought they would
> create a new person out of me. When I eventually
> realized that commercials were just commercials
> and they could not change or shape me, it was too
> late. I had been taken advantage of. (Haley G.)

Works Cited

G., Haley. "Teens and Advertising." *SNN Student Magazine* Nov. 2002
    <http:72.14.205.104/search?q=cache:K52Hiu-wGIUJ:www.snn-rdr.ca/
    sn…ov/advertising.html+advertising+%2B+teens&hl=en&ct=clnk&cd=6&gl
    =ca>.

Heyman, David. "TV, Movies Can Harm Children's Health—Doctors." *The
    Edmonton Journal* 20 June 2003: 15.

"Impact of Media Use on Children and Youth: Television." Psychosocial
    Paediatrics Committee, Canadian Paediatric Society (CPS).
    <http:www.cps.ca/English/statements/PP/pp03-01.htm>.

Kirkey, Sharon. "A Nation off the Wagon." *The Edmonton Journal* 17 Dec.
    2007: A3.

"Marketing and Consumerism—Overview." Media Awareness Network. 2007.
    <http://www.media-awareness.ca/english/parents/marketing/index.cfm>.

Media Awareness Network and the Canadian Paediatric Society.
    MediaPulse: Measuring the Media in Kids' Lives. Ottawa: 2003.

Schor, Juliet B. *Born to Buy.* Toronto: Scribner, 2004.

Tamzarian, Armen. "Little Pitchers Have Big Ears—and Bellies." *National
    Review of Medicine* 1.7 (2004) 15 April 2004 <http://www.
    nationalreviewofmedicine.com/issue/2004_04_15/feature14_07.htm>.

Business Writing

E-mail

E-mail can be formal or informal. Specifically, the term refers to the electronic correspondence between two or more parties.

E-mail Features and Etiquette

- First names and a friendly, positive tone are acceptable in most e-mails (for example, *Hi, Marla,* or *See you later, Jai*).

- Missing words, misspelled words, and errors in grammar are not acceptable.

- Many users don't like attachment files, mass e-mailings, and unsolicited e-mail.

- E-mail should not be too personal or angry in tone. For example, the use of capital letters for entire words is interpreted as shouting.

- If your e-mail is urgent, the Subject heading in most e-mail programs allows you to indicate this.

Sample E-mail

To: ychang@abcd.net
From: bmcginitie@efgh.net
Date: Wed, 1 Sep 20__ 20:01:04-0600 (MDT)
Subject: Benefit Concert Acts

Attachments: [Indicates whether you have a file attached to the message]

Yuan,

I have a concern with the order of the acts in the benefit performance next week. Perhaps we should be ending the show on a bigger note, a large group rather than a solo. What do you think?

Regards,
Becky

Many job opportunities require applicants to submit a résumé. Unlike an application form, which requires you to supply only the most basic information, a résumé allows you to provide a personalized, comprehensive, and organized overview of your experience and qualifications. This level of detail helps an employer choose which applicants to interview.

Résumés include standard information, such as your name and address, as well as specific information about your education and experience.

Personal Data

Name

Address

Postal code

Phone number

Fax number (if applicable)

E-mail address (if applicable)

Summary of Skills and Qualifications

- List any job-related skills gained at home or through part-time work, such as using computer software, operating a cash register, answering telephones, stocking shelves, setting up displays, or taking inventory.

- List hobbies, club memberships, and volunteer experience, as well as languages other than English that you can speak and/or write. Some résumés (such as the one on pages 136–137) give separate lists of skills, organizations, volunteer experience, and interests.

Work Experience

Dates of employment (most recent first)

Position, Employer/Company

Duties

Repeat this information for every job you have had. If you have little or no work experience, include other areas of responsibility, such as babysitting, counselling, volunteer work, or student council work.

Education

List the school you are attending, the grade level you have completed, and your current grade level.

References

Provide the names of two or three previous employers, teachers, or people who know you well. (Do not list friends or relatives as references.) Choose people who can confirm the accuracy of the information you have provided in your résumé. Be sure to ask these people if you can use them as references before you list their names.

You may either list your references or state *Available upon request,* as in the sample résumé that follows. For each reference, provide the following information:

Name

Position, Company

Address with postal code

Phone number

E-mail address

Format

Leave some space between sections of your résumé and either underline or boldface the headings. Each section should be clear and easy to read.

Paula Gonzales
#840—978 Twelfth Street, Clearview, Alberta, T7Z 3W7
(123) 456-7890   paulagon@abcd.net

Summary of Skills and Qualifications

– Excellent oral and written communication skills

– Fluency in Portuguese

– Experience in handling cash transactions and in preparing fast food

– Proven ability to deal with customers in a friendly and flexible manner

– Superior organizational and interpersonal skills

– Proficiency in Macintosh and PC computer applications, including Microsoft Word and Excel, Adobe Acrobat, Computer-Aided Design, and Internet-related functions

– Musical aptitude (bass clarinet, guitar, and piano)

Work Experience

December 2007 to present

Weekend Supervisor, Bowled Over

Involved in the maintenance and operation of a 12-lane bowling alley. Duties include operating the sound system, distributing and disinfecting rental shoes, and operating an admission and concession area.

July to August 2007

Junior Associate, Wilson's Housewares

Was part of the set-up crew for the construction of a new store. Duties included setting up store fixtures, stocking shelves and other storage spaces, preparing the garden centre, and arranging displays.

Organizations

– Atom/Bantam Hockey League: October 2006 to present

– J. K. Strong Concert, Dixieland, and Jazz Bands: September 2006 to present

Volunteer Experience

December 2006 and 2007
Clearview Cancer Society
Stuffed envelopes for the annual campaign

Summer 2006 and 2007
Wilson's Golf Tournament, Clearview Public Golf Course
Provided caddy service and prepared golf carts

Interests

I enjoy composing and playing music, and filling in as a guitarist in my cousin's band. I keep active playing soccer, working out, bowling, and skating with my friends. In my spare time, I enjoy using the home computer for both work and entertainment.

Education

J. K. Strong Composite High School
Grade 9 completed, now in grade 10

References

Available upon request

When you apply for a job, include a cover letter, or letter of application, along with your résumé. As with most business letters, cover letters are formatted in full-block style (all the text is aligned at the left margin). Although it is preferable to input your cover letter, a handwritten letter is acceptable if it is neat and legible.

Most cover letters consist of the following nine elements, which are featured in the sample letter on the facing page.

1. The complete address of the sender (the applicant) is placed about 2.5 cm down the page and at the left margin, one line under the other, with no indent. Below this is the date when the letter was written.

2. The name and address of the person who should receive the letter and résumé comes next. (Note that there is no end punctuation in either address on the letter.)

3. The letter opens with a formal greeting (usually *Dear* ___) followed by a colon.

4. The first paragraph expresses interest in the job and states how the applicant found out about it. (Note that with full-block style, the paragraphs are not indented, but there is an extra line space between them.)

5. The second paragraph highlights experience relevant to the job.

6. The third paragraph refers to the enclosed résumé and outlines contact information.

7. The letter ends with a courteous closing, along with the sender's signature.

8. The sender's full name is keyed in below the signature. (For a handwritten letter, the name is printed below the signature.)

9. Below the sender's name is an abbreviation of the word *enclosure* (Encl.) or the word *attachment* (Att.). Either abbreviation can be used to indicate that there are other documents accompanying the letter, namely the résumé.

#840—978 Twelfth Street
Clearview, Alberta
T7Z 3W7
(123) 456-7890
paulagon@abcd.net

February 27, 2008

Mr. Malcolm O'Donnell
Clearview Public Golf Course
Clearview, Alberta
T7T 6N5

Dear Mr. O'Donnell:

I am writing to show my interest in the position of apprentice groundskeeper advertised in the February 24 Business section of the *Clearview Clarion.* My physical education teacher, Ms. Sharon Kucenik, is a member of your club, and she suggested that I would be a suitable candidate for the job.

I enjoy golf very much, and for the past two summers I have volunteered at your annual Wilson's Golf Tournament. I would like to get to know all aspects of the sport, and I believe that my experience with golf makes me the perfect match for the position advertised. I am conscientious, well organized, and eager to learn as much as I can.

Please see my enclosed résumé and letter of reference from Ms. Kucenik. I am home by 5 p.m. on weekdays and can be reached there by phone. If you prefer, you may also contact me by e-mail at paulagon@abcd.net.

Thank you for your consideration and I look forward to hearing from you.

Sincerely,

Paula Gonzales

Paula Gonzales

Encl. (résumé, letter of reference)

A letter of invitation can be brief and straightforward, or slightly longer, depending on the occasion and the recipient. In the sample below, the student is working for his school's student council and has been assigned the task of writing a letter to parents, inviting them to come to the annual Awards Night.

Sample Invitation Letter

Main High School
122 Russell Street
Halifax, Nova Scotia, B3J 2S9

May 30, 2008

Mr. and Mrs. S. Singh
332 Woodlands Avenue
Halifax, Nova Scotia
B3M 2N1

Dear Mr. and Mrs. Singh:

On June 16, Main High School will host its annual Awards Night. You are cordially invited to attend the ceremony, which will honour the school's most outstanding achievers.

The evening will pay tribute to 102 students who have excelled in the areas of academics, participation, leadership, and athletics. The evening will also feature a brief performance by Ragged Edge, our school band.

The evening will begin at 7:00 p.m. and end at approximately 9:30 p.m. Please call Ms. Helena Dubois, our school secretary, at 555-3333, to confirm your attendance.

I hope you will join me on June 16 to celebrate Main High School's best and brightest.

Sincerely,

Stephen Meisner

Stephen Meisner
Class Representative

Thank-you Letter

Thank-you letters express appreciation to others for gifts they have given or services they have provided. This type of letter tends to be brief and straightforward.

Sample | Thank-you Letter

Main High School
122 Russell Street
Halifax, Nova Scotia, B3J 2S9

June 19, 2008

Mr. Anthony Musante
217 Shorelands Drive
Halifax, Nova Scotia
B2Y 3C5

Dear Mr. Musante:

I am writing on behalf of the Main High School Student Council to express our thanks for your contribution to our Awards Night. Your speech was appropriately inspiring and memorable. Thank you for helping to make this a special evening for all.

Sincerely,

Stephen Meisner

Stephen Meisner
Class Representative

A letter of request asks an individual or an organization for a favour. Provide sufficient detail in the letter so that the person reading it understands what you require. The letter should include your contact information in case the recipient has questions or concerns.

Main High School
122 Russell Street
Halifax, Nova Scotia, B3J 2S9

April 30, 2008

Advertising Manager
X-treme Artworks Ltd.
123 Brinks Avenue
Vancouver, British Columbia
V6H 3C7

To Whom It May Concern:

The drama department at Main High School is interested in purchasing several of your vintage-era movie posters. These will be used as set decorations in our upcoming theatre production.

Would you please send me your catalogue of poster titles and prices? As we are on a limited budget, any price reduction that you can give us would be appreciated. We would gladly mention your assistance in our printed program.

If you require additional information, you can reach me at the school at (902) 555-3333, or e-mail me at mkalinowski@mnop.net.

Sincerely,

Maxine Kalinowski

Maxine Kalinowski
Student Representative
Main High School Drama Department

Speech

Getting Started

If you're asked to give a speech, begin by doing the following:

- Decide on the topic if you're given a choice, or identify what aspect(s) of the assigned topic you will address.

- Establish a clear purpose for writing the speech. Your purpose should take into account the audience to whom you will present your speech. For example, do you need to explain the conflict in a play to your English class, or persuade a group of community leaders to support your school's fundraising drive?

- Jot down ideas and details you might include in your speech.

- Do any necessary research. Gather information that will be both useful and interesting to your audience.

- Find some relevant and meaningful quotations to include in your speech.

Preparing Your Speech

Follow these guidelines as you prepare your speech:

- Keep your audience in mind. What will interest them? What do they need to know? (You may have to present some background to the topic first.)

- Organize your work in an easy-to-follow, logical manner using clear transitions that lead from one idea or detail to the next. Include an introduction and a conclusion.

- Include something memorable at the beginning to get your audience's attention, and at the end to keep them thinking about what you have said. For example, you might share a brief, humorous anecdote that captures their attention, or recount a personal experience that reinforces your message.

- Provide specific examples to help your listeners understand the points you are making.

- Avoid jargon whenever possible, and explain any specialized or technical words that you decide you must include.

- Include visual aids such as maps, photos, and charts, and make use of technology when possible (overhead projector,

PowerPoint). Ensure any visual aids you use are clear and easy to read, free of spelling errors, and in the right order.

- Use appropriate humour, avoiding jokes that are silly or offensive.

Tips for Presenting Your Speech

Copy your speech onto one or more index cards or sheets of paper (numbered in sequence). You can either copy the whole speech or just a point-form version of it. Below is an example of point-form notes for a speech on how to research a family tree.

How can someone research his or her family tree?
Interview living relatives.
Check family photographs.
Check birth and marriage certificates.
Do research online and at the library.
Benefits of family-tree research

Using a point-form copy of your speech will enable you to maintain eye contact with your audience and actually deliver your speech rather than just read it aloud word-for-word.

Here are some other strategies that will help to make your presentation as successful as possible:

- Rehearse your speech alone or in front of one or more people. You might also practise delivering your speech in front of a mirror or, if available, into an audio recorder or in front of a video camera. Rehearse your speech until your words flow naturally and you can include appropriate gestures and facial expressions.

- Stand with your weight evenly distributed on both feet. If your weight is more on one foot, you will shift frequently during the speech, which can be distracting to your audience.

- Before you begin to speak, take a deep breath and exhale. Glance down at your notes and then look up at the audience and begin.

- Speak loudly and clearly so that the people sitting farthest away from you can hear you. Do not yell, however.

- Vary the pitch of your voice. Do not speak in a monotone.

- Try to make eye contact with the whole audience. Don't forget the people sitting at the sides and back of the room.

- Open your speech by acknowledging your audience and end by thanking them for listening to you.

- Pace your delivery so that listeners can process what you are saying. To signal to your audience that a change in content or direction is coming, stress transitional words and phrases such as *first, in addition,* or *finally.*

- Pause briefly after complicated or important points to give your audience time to think about what you're saying.

- Avoid fillers such as *uh* or *eh.*

If you can show that you're interested in and enthusiastic about your topic, your audience will be much more likely to listen attentively and respect what you have to say.

Speeches and fruit should
always be fresh.

Nikki Giovanni

Oral Presentation

An oral presentation involves much more than simply reading aloud a piece of writing. With the technology that is now available, presentations can be elaborate events. Most oral presentations of any complexity tend to be done by pairs or small groups. With this in mind, you need to consider these questions.

What is the purpose of the presentation?

Understand clearly what you are being asked to do. Research and organize the material as you would any longer form of writing, such as an essay or research paper. Whether your main purpose is to inform, entertain, persuade, or explain something to your audience, approach your topic from their perspective. What you plan to say should satisfy the audience's reason for coming to listen to you.

Who is the audience, and what are their expectations?

If your audience consists of your teacher and classmates, address them appropriately as individuals you work with every day and know well. If your audience is outside your classroom, consider their needs and interests. Fine-tune your content, diction, and manner of presentation to suit your audience.

How should the responsibilities be shared?

It's usually best if all group members work together on the presentation as a whole, at least initially. Rather than dividing the topic into parts for each group member to complete independently, discuss each part as a group. As much as possible, work together to brainstorm, collect information, and even write some of the content, encouraging everyone to contribute ideas. This will ensure the unity of the presentation and make it that much more effective.

Once you have established the content, decide how you will present it to your audience. Will each speaker simply follow another from first to last, or would it be better for all to be involved throughout, moving back and forth from speaker to speaker? Would some group members prefer to present certain sections, perhaps because they have a deeper knowledge of a particular research source? Are some group members more proficient with certain types of presentation technology than others?

Regardless of how you finally divide up the tasks involved, do your best to ensure that each group member has an equal chance to contribute and present.

How much time do you have to present?
Be clear about how much time you have to present and then prepare sufficient material to fill about three-quarters of that time. (Allow about one-quarter of the total time for questions and discussion at the end of the presentation.) Pace your presentation carefully. If you and your group present too quickly, the audience may become confused. If you present too slowly, you may lose the attention of your listeners.

Where will the presentation take place?
Try to visit the site for your presentation in advance so that you can plan accordingly. How big is the room? If it's a large room, like an auditorium, is sound amplification available? Will your audience be seated? Will most seats be filled? How will the seats be arranged (for example, in rows or around the edge of the room)? Where will your presentation group be sitting or standing (for example, will you be behind a table facing the audience, or on a stage)? Will you be able to move among your audience and present from different areas in the room?

Finding answers to these questions in advance of your presentation will help you to make the best possible use of the physical space and conditions available. If possible, try to hold one or two practice sessions in the actual room to be used for the final presentation.

> **Tips for Highlighting Ideas in Your Presentation**
>
> - State your thesis early, and then restate it once or twice during your presentation.
>
> - Use transitional devices, such as *most important*, *first*, *next*, and *another*, to highlight key points or to signal to the audience that you're moving from one subtopic to the next.
>
> - Display subtopic headings using an overhead projector, or list them on a flipchart.
>
> - Summarize different sections after you've presented them.

Refer to pages 144 and 145 for tips on body language and pacing during your presentation.

What kinds of visual aids or presentation technology will be available and permitted? Which would best enhance your particular presentation?

We live in a very visual world, which means that audiences expect information to be presented visually as well as through the spoken word. Don't simply use visual aids or presentation technology for their own sake, however. Select only what will enhance your delivery, and then plan your presentation based on what equipment is available (for example, overhead projectors and flipcharts). Bear in mind the following:

- Flipcharts give you two advantages: they allow you to prepare material in advance and give you the option of adding to them while you're speaking. Remember, though, that flipcharts can be difficult to read from a distance.

- Overhead transparencies can serve a large space. You can also write on them during your presentation, if necessary. They require a somewhat darkened room, however, which could make it difficult for your audience to take notes.

- Electronic and digital slideshow equipment such as PowerPoint and digitized graphs and photographs are highly effective presentation aids. Properly used, they can be visually stunning and highly motivational. Unfortunately, you cannot write on them during your presentation as you can with overhead transparencies.

- Videotaped film clips add interest, but you should use only short sequences so that the video component doesn't dominate the presentation.

Tips for Electronic Presentations

- Don't try to cram too much information onto slides; three or four bulleted points along with a visual work best.

- Don't use too many slides: 25 or 30 are generally sufficient.

- Use a large font, such as 36 point for heads and 24 point for text.

- Run through the presentation once or twice to identify and fix any technological problems.

When using visual aids, it's important to remember that they are a supplement to your presentation. They should not simply repeat what you have already said or replace what you need to say convincingly yourself.

Writing for Assessment

For the purpose of assessment, you may be required to generate one or more forms of writing within a limited period of time—perhaps just an hour or so. These assessment opportunities provide little time for you to plan, organize, revise, edit, and proofread your work. To be able to write successfully under pressure, you must be focussed and able to organize your ideas quickly.

Below are some suggestions for dealing with such assessment situations.

Situation	*Suggestions*
You have to respond to a question or a prompt.	• Read the question or prompt carefully more than once to make sure you understand what it's asking you to do. • If the question has more than one part, number and answer each part. • Make sure you understand the purpose for the writing and the audience for whom you're writing. • Underline all key words in the question or prompt. Below are some common key words to look for, along with suggestions for how to respond to them. *Compare*: Show how two people or two things are similar to and different from each other, with an emphasis on similarities. *Contrast*: Show how two people or two things are different from each other. *Define*: State the meaning of something. *Describe*: Give the physical characteristics of someone or something. *Discuss*: Write about different aspects of a topic.

Explain: Make clear what something is like, how something works, or why something happens.

Illustrate: Provide supporting details and evidence, including visuals such as diagrams, as appropriate.

Justify or *Prove*: Give reasons or evidence to show why an answer or argument is correct.

Summarize: Concisely identify the main idea or ideas included in an original text.

- Check any unfamiliar words in a dictionary, if permissible.
- Restate the instructions in your own words. Often, the question or prompt can be reworded to create a topic sentence for a single-paragraph answer or as a thesis statement for a longer piece of writing. If the task requires selecting one side of an issue, decide which side you'll take and then state that position clearly in your own words.

You have a very limited amount of time to plan.

- Block some time for planning and stick to this time limit. For example, if you have only an hour to write something, take at least ten minutes to jot down ideas and plan.
- Create a brief outline. Include only the best ideas and subtopics you jotted down, arranged in the order in which you'll deal with them in your writing.

You have to give a personal opinion or write a personal response.

- Write in the first person.
- Think of links between the topic and your own knowledge and personal experiences.
- Mention any relevant experiences or observations of those closest to you, such as family members or friends.

	• Refer to a relevant book, movie, or television show that deals with the same or a similar topic.
	• Support your views and observations with reasons and relevant examples or facts.
You're not sure what to put in the introduction.	• Mention the topic and state your thesis.
	• Develop your introduction by writing a sentence for each of the subtopics listed in your outline.
You're not sure what to put in the conclusion.	• Restate the thesis in some way.
	• Leave your reader with something to remember, such as a vivid image, a question to ponder, a strongly stated opinion, or a call to action.
You have a very limited amount of time to revise, edit, and proofread.	• Block some time for revising, editing, and proofreading, and stick to this time limit. For example, if you have only an hour to write something, allow at least ten minutes to complete these three stages of the writing process.
	• When you're finished, carefully read over what you have written. If a sentence sounds awkward, rewrite it. Make sure all sentences are complete and can stand alone.
	• Make sure that verb tenses are consistent and that all pronouns have clear antecedent references.
	• Check the context for homophones to be sure you've spelled them correctly.
	• Check for incorrect spellings.
	• Review your use of apostrophes. Are they needed, and are they placed correctly?
	• If you have time, add brief transitions such as *in fact, therefore,* and *however* as necessary.

- Replace any vague words such as *good, nice,* and *great* with more precise ones.
- Delete anything that is repetitious, contradictory, or irrelevant to the topic.

You need to add or delete information at the last moment.

- Add any necessary information using numbered notes. Write the extra information neatly at the bottom of the page, in the margins, or on the reverse side of the page if it's blank. Keep such added information to a minimum.
- Delete words or phrases neatly, using single horizontal lines. Indicate a longer section of text to be deleted by marking an X through it, or by enclosing it in square brackets and writing *delete* in the margin. Keep deletions to a minimum.

You fail only if you stop writing.

Ray Bradbury

Part 4

Conventions of Writing

Sentences

A sentence is a group of words that expresses a complete thought. For your writing to be effective, keep in mind the following eight aspects of sentence construction:

- **clearness**

  No part of a sentence should be awkward or unclear. If you think that a sentence will be unclear to a reader, rewrite it.

  While eating lunch, the rain began to fall.

  should be

  While I was eating lunch, the rain began to fall.

- **completeness**

  If you read a sentence aloud and it sounds incomplete, it probably is. Check for the following error:

  – sentence fragments

    While smiling at the camera

    is a fragment (a piece) of a sentence. It needs a subject and a verb to complete it.

    While smiling at the camera, the boy backed toward the car.

    or

    The boy backed toward the car while smiling at the camera.

- **correct punctuation**

  A sentence always ends with a period, a question mark, or an exclamation mark. Be careful about the following:

  – comma splices

    You need to exercise your muscles or they will become weak, the same advice applies to the brain.

    This construction attempts to join, or splice, two sentences together using only a comma. The simplest ways to correct this are to create two separate sentences, or to add a conjunction such as *and*.

    You need to exercise your muscles or they will become weak. The same advice applies to the brain.

    or

    You need to exercise your muscles or they will become weak, and the same advice applies to the brain.

You could also replace the comma with a semicolon.

You need to exercise your muscles or they will become weak; the same advice applies to the brain.

– run-on (or fused) sentences

I need to exercise more I am joining a workout group.

This is similar to a comma splice. Now, though, two sentences run together, without even a comma between them. The three ways to correct run-on sentences are the same as for correcting commas splices: create separate sentences, add a conjunction, or use a semicolon.

I need to exercise more. I am joining a workout group.

I need to exercise more so I am joining a workout group.

I need to exercise more; I am joining a workout group.

- **consistent verb tenses**
Present and past tense verbs should not be mixed in the same sentence.

She blurted out the answer and then immediately turns red.

should be changed to one of the following:

She blurted out the answer and then immediately turned red.

or

She blurts out the answer and then immediately turns red.

- **subject agreement**
  – subject-verb agreement

  The principal verb must be the same in number (singular or plural) as the subject of the sentence. This is not the case in the following example.

  This recent chain of events are surprising.

  Because the subject *chain* is singular, the singular form of the verb applies (*is* not *are*).

  This recent chain of events is surprising.

  – noun and pronoun agreement/clarity

  A pronoun must relate in number to its antecedent, the noun to which it refers. This is not the case in the following example.

  Each of the girls in my class had completed their homework.

Here, the noun antecedent of the pronoun is *each*, not *girls*. Therefore, the pronoun must be singular (*her* not *their*).

Each of the girls in my class had completed her homework.

A pronoun's noun antecedent must be very clear.

My friend likes playing hockey with his brother because he is so good.

should be changed to

My friend likes playing hockey with his brother because his brother is so good.

Be careful. The farther away a verb or a pronoun is from its subject, the easier it is to make an error in agreement or clarity.

- **parallel structure in series**
  Parallel ideas should be presented in parallel sentence structures.

  She hoped to finish her essay, that she would print it, and she could submit it the next day.

  should be changed to

  She hoped to finish her essay, to print it, and to submit it the next day.

- **variety in sentence types and lengths**
  It's tedious to read a sequence of sentences that are structured similarly.

  This scene shows Janice and Mahmood playfully throwing snow at each other. This scene also proves Janice is interested in Mahmood.

  Try the following ways to avoid writing one simple sentence after another:

  – Combine simple sentences to create compound sentences.

    This scene shows Janice and Mahmood playfully throwing snow at each other, and that Janice is interested in Mahmood.

  – Start the sentence with a transitional word.

    Clearly, the playful snow-throwing scene shows that Janice is interested in Mahmood.

  – Start the sentence with a phrase.

    In the playful snow-throwing scene, it's clear that Janice is interested in Mahmood.

– Start the sentence with a subordinate clause.

When Janice and Mahmood are playfully throwing snow at each other, it's clear that she is interested in him.

– Vary the lengths of your sentences for effect.

When Janice and Mahmood are playfully throwing snow at each other, it's clear that Janice isn't acting any more. She likes him.

- **sentence combining**
One way to add variety and interest to your sentences is to combine sentences. This technique also helps you to reduce the number of words. In sentence combining, you first eliminate any words that are repeated in a sequence of sentences. Then you combine the important ideas into a single sentence. Consider the following examples:

The reporters were from the National News Service. They had arrived to question the premier.

In this example, 15 words in two sentences can be reduced to 13 in one sentence without losing any meaning:

The reporters from the National News Service had arrived to question the premier.

The following four sentences contain a total of 18 words:

We were in the locker room. It was half-time. Our coach outlined the strategy. She did it carefully.

When the four sentences are combined into one sentence, the total number of words drops to 12.

In the locker room at half-time, our coach carefully outlined the strategy.

Diction

Good diction—choosing the right word—will add clarity to your writing. For example, if you're talking about a character's life, it would be more informative to say his or her life is *tragic* (which suggests suffering and misfortune) than to say his or her life is *sad* (which is vague).

How do you decide which word to choose? Here are some strategies to help you:

Be specific.
Replace vague words with words that are specific. For example, *Manuel was nice to John* is not nearly as specific as *Manuel was helpful to John.*

Use a thesaurus.
A thesaurus—a book of synonyms—can help you come up with the best word to use. However, it is important to then check the meaning of that word in a dictionary to confirm it is appropriate for your sentence. For the vague word *interesting*, here are some of the synonyms that are listed in the thesaurus: *captivating, fascinating, intriguing, striking, unusual.* Each of these words is clearer and more precise in meaning than *interesting.*

If you are writing dialogue for a story, instead of using the verb *said* repeatedly, consider more specific verbs such as *answered, whispered, divulged,* and *implied.*

Be cautious of using a thesaurus simply to drop multi-syllabic words into your writing. For example, you might be tempted to replace the word *fun* with *jocularity* in an attempt to impress your reader. However, your writing may come across as artificial or insincere. It's better to spend your time trying to clarify your thoughts. Focus on trying to use clear, honest, and precise communication.

Avoid clichés.
Clichés are stale, unoriginal, lazy ways of saying something, and they can be found in all types of communication. Here are just a few examples: *start from scratch; the big picture; get away from it all; food for thought; live life to the fullest; face the music; our backs to the wall; give 110 percent; it's not over till it's over.* The best way to avoid clichés in your writing is to think carefully about what you are trying to say, and then use simple, straightforward language to say it.

Avoid euphemisms.

A euphemism is a word or phrase that is used in place of words or phrases that may be considered harsh, unpleasant, or offensive. In some situations, such as when referring to someone who has died, using a euphemism might be appropriate. Some common euphemisms include *pass away* for *die, act up* for *misbehave, pre-owned* for *used,* and *correctional facility* for *prison.* As a general rule, however, avoid euphemisms in your writing.

Avoid informal language or slang in formal writing.

Informal words and expressions are acceptable in most conversations, in very informal writing (such as some e-mails and letters), and in scripts. They are not, however, acceptable in formal writing, unless used sparingly and placed inside quotation marks to identify them as informal. Examples include *No problem, Get with it,* and *Get real.*

Slang refers to very informal words and expressions used by individuals of a particular age or group. Examples include *brutal* for *bad, 411* for *information,* and *awesome* for *impressive.* Slang should not be used in most writing, unless identified as the words said by a particular person, as in dialogue.

Avoid redundancy.

Redundancy is the use of unnecessary or needlessly repeated words in a sentence. Removing the unnecessary words from

The reason why he speaks in this way is because he is enthusiastic.

results in

He speaks in this way because he is enthusiastic.

Examples of needless repetition include *continue on* for *continue, repeat again* for *repeat, over-exaggerate* for *exaggerate,* and *very unique* for *unique.*

A sentence should contain no unnecessary words, a paragraph no unnecessary sentences, for the same reason that a drawing should have no unnecessary lines and a machine no unnecessary parts.

William Strunk, Jr.

Use the correct verb voice.

A verb is in the active voice if its subject is the doer of the action.

The firefighters extinguished the fire.

A verb is in the passive voice when the subject of the verb receives the action.

The fire was extinguished by the firefighters.

The passive voice allows the doer of the action to be left out if necessary, leaving the doer either unknown or obvious, or suggesting that the doer is unimportant. To stress objectivity, writers of objective pieces such as scientific papers often prefer the passive voice.

A flame was applied to the compound to achieve the necessary result.

Don't use *I*, *we*, or *you* in formal writing.

Unless you are writing a narrative or a personal essay, avoid using *I*. In formal writing, avoid using *we* in place of *everyone*.

We know that there is a right way and a wrong way to behave.

should be

Everyone knows that there is a right way and a wrong way to behave.

Also in formal writing, avoid using *you* in place of *people*.

You should always eat nutritious food.

should be

People should always eat nutritious food.

Don't use double negatives.

Using two negative words such as *not* and *never* in the same sentence creates a double negative. Often, double negatives occur in sentences that include the word *not* as part of a contraction (for example, *can't*, *won't*, *shouldn't*). Avoid confusion by removing or replacing one of the two negatives.

They can't never get that straight.

should be changed to one of the following:

They can never get that straight.

They cannot ever get that straight.

Avoid biassed language.

Avoid language that could be interpreted as biassed on the basis of sex, age, physical ability, or ethnic or racial identity.

Don't use racist language.

Racist language is any language that refers to a particular ethnic or cultural background in over-generalized and often insulting terms. Here are three ways to avoid such language:

- Mention a person's ethnic or cultural background only if doing so is relevant to the context:

✗ irrelevant	✓
A [adjective identifying ethnic or cultural background] *woman has been charged after a store was deliberately set on fire.*	*A woman has been charged after a store was deliberately set on fire.*

- If a person's ethnic or cultural background is relevant, be as specific as possible:

✗ vague	✓
He emigrated from Asia.	*He emigrated from Tokyo.*

- Avoid making generalizations about any ethnic or cultural group:

✗ vague	✓
The French are excellent cooks.	*France is noted for its fine dining.*

Don't use sexist language.

There are several ways to avoid sexist wording.

• If the person's gender is not known, use *a* or *the* with a noun instead of *his* or *her*.

The doctor knows his patient well.

should be

The doctor knows the patient well.

• You can also use plural forms.

Doctors know their patients well.

• Use a thesaurus to find non-sexist replacements that include both genders:

✗ non-inclusive	✓ gender-inclusive
man, mankind	*human(kind), human beings, humanity, the human race, people*
manpower	*workers, personnel*
workman	*worker*
chairman, chairwoman	*chairperson, chair*
policeman	*police officer, law enforcement officer*
postman, mailman	*mail carrier, letter carrier*
fireman	*firefighter*
stewardess	*flight attendant*
weatherman	*meteorologist*
mothering	*parenting*

Build your vocabulary.

People often judge others by their language. Using dull, immature, or inappropriate language in writing will leave a poor impression on your reader. On the other hand, having a wide selection of words from which to choose will enable you to speak, think, write, and communicate more effectively.

Here are some strategies for building your vocabulary:

- Read books, magazines, or e-zines (electronic magazines) on subjects that interest you.
- Take a book or other reading material with you when you are waiting for an appointment.
- Look up unfamiliar words or terms in a dictionary.
- Read a dictionary, even a page at a time.
- Use a print or online thesaurus to look up synonyms or antonyms.
- Browse bookstores.
- Take notes in class. Exchange and discuss them with other classmates.
- Rewrite unsuccessful assignments. Ask your teacher if these can be re-marked.
- Enter writing competitions at your school, in newspapers or magazines, or online.
- Keep a journal or blog.
- Write poetry.
- Talk to friends about the books, magazines, and e-zines you read.
- Talk to friends about movies, and read movie reviews.
- Write letters or send e-mails to friends and family members.
- Try word quizzes like those found in magazines and on websites.
- Try doing crosswords and word searches.
- Play a word game such as Scrabble.
- Watch game shows such as *Jeopardy* that can expand your vocabulary and general knowledge.
- Watch specialized television shows, such as biographies, science and nature programs, or history-related television. Note the specialized terms and phrases unique to these shows.

COMMONLY CONFUSED WORDS

A/An

A is used before nouns starting with consonants.
*Ravi had **a** dream of becoming successful.*

An is used before nouns starting with vowels.
*Susanna ate **an** apple.*

Accept/Except

Accept is a verb meaning *receive*.
*The actor will **accept** the award from the academy.*

Except is usually a preposition meaning *other than*.
*Everyone **except** John is going to university.*

Advice/Advise

Advice is a noun referring to *that which is given*.
*The counsellor gave **advice** to the students about their options.*

Advise is a verb meaning *to counsel*.
*The counsellor will **advise** students about the choices they should be making.*

Allusion/Illusion

Allusion means *reference to something that is well known*.
On The Simpsons *there was an **allusion** to J.K. Rowling's character Harry Potter.*

Illusion means *false idea*.
*The mirage created the **illusion** of water on the desert horizon.*

Already/All ready

Already is an adjective meaning *by this time*.
*It is **already** too late in the day to go to the beach.*

All ready is an adverb meaning *completely ready*.
*The sprinter was **all ready** for her event.*

Alright/All right

Alright is the informal spelling of *all right*. It should be avoided in formal writing.
*The prime minister said it was **all right** to start the debate.*

Altogether/All together

Altogether means *completely* or *all things considered*.
***Altogether**, there were four touchdowns scored in the game.*

All together emphasizes *all things or people in a group*.
*The teachers brought the students **all together** in the gym.*

Among/Between

Among implies *more than two people or things*.
*There are many celebrities scattered **among** the large crowd.*

Between refers to *only two in number*.
*Carlos and I split the chips **between** us.*

Amount/Number

Amount is used to refer to *something in a mass.*
> We ordered a large **amount** of topsoil for the garden.

Number is used to refer to *individual, countable items.*
> We ordered a large **number** of plants for the garden.

Assure/Ensure/Insure

Assure means *restore confidence.*
> The doctor will **assure** you that you are healthy.

Ensure means *make certain or safe.*
> A working smoke detector can **ensure** the safety of your family.

Insure means *arrange to be paid in case of damage or theft.*
> You ought to **insure** your house, car, and other valuables.

Bare/Bear

Bare is often an adjective meaning *uncovered* or *empty.*
> **Bare** skin freezes quickly in Arctic conditions.

> After they removed all the furniture, the room was **bare**.

Bear is either a noun referring to *a large, furry mammal,* or a verb meaning *to put up with.*
> Facing a grizzly **bear** so soon after a cougar attack was more than I could **bear**.

Beside/Besides

Beside means *by the side of.*
> The grass **beside** the fence needs cutting.

Besides means *in addition to.*
> Who is coming **besides** us?

Board/Bored

Board is usually a noun referring to *wood, a group of people,* or *a wall surface used for writing.*
> Hammer the nail into that piece of **board**.

> Each school **board** member wrote his or her name on the white **board**.

Bored is the past tense of the verb *bore,* and means *tired* or *uninterested.*
> The audience became **bored** listening to the speaker go on and on.

Brake/Break

Brake is commonly used in its noun form, referring to *a device for stopping the motion of a moving object.*
> Step lightly on your car **brake** when approaching an intersection.

Break is most often used as a verb meaning *damage,* or as a noun meaning *pause* or *welcome change in activity.*
> The child may **break** the toy if she continues to play roughly with it.

> The professor gave her class a coffee **break** to discuss the upcoming spring **break**.

Breath/Breathe

Breath is a noun referring to *air that is inhaled.*
> Take a deep **breath**.

Breathe is a verb referring to *the action of inhaling,* or *drawing in air.*
> **Breathe** normally while the doctor listens to your lungs.

Buy/By

Buy is a verb meaning *purchase*.
When you start your first job, you can **buy** *your own clothes.*

By is a preposition meaning *beside* or *through the act of*.
He was standing **by** *the car pumping gas.*

Jurassic Park, *directed* **by** *Steven Spielberg, has become a film classic.*

Can/May

Can means *able to*.
You **can** *do a great deal to help improve the situation.*

May suggests *possibility, opportunity,* or *permission*.
It **may** *snow soon.* **May** *I leave now?*

Choose/Chose/Choice

These three terms are often confused in pronunciation and spelling.
Choose is a present tense verb, *chose* is a past tense verb, and *choice* is a noun.
Choose *your words carefully.*

I **chose** *to finish the course.*

Ian had to make a difficult **choice**.

Complement/Compliment

Complement refers to *something that completes or makes perfect*.
The team was finally able to dress its full **complement** *of players.*

Compliment refers to *an expression of praise for someone or something*.
The teacher planned to **compliment** *his students for their efforts.*

Conscience/Conscious

Conscience is a noun meaning *awareness of right or wrong*.
The criminal had no **conscience** *about his crimes.*

Conscious is an adjective meaning *aware*.
Miko was not **conscious** *of the cat in the window.*

Could have/Could of

Of should never follow *could* to replace the contraction *could've*, which is short for the formally correct *could have*.
Jaswant **could have** *e-mailed his cousin last night.*

Council/Counsel

Council is a noun referring to *a group of people elected or appointed to give advice*.
Jackson was elected president of the student **council**.

Counsel can be used as a verb meaning *advise*, or as a noun meaning a *lawyer*.
A good coach will **counsel** *her players to become better citizens as well as athletes.*

He is the best defence **counsel** *in the city.*

Couple/Few/Several

Couple always refers to *two in number.*
> A **couple** *of months went by before their subscription expired.*

Few may refer specifically to *three,* or not many more than three.
> A **few** *players preferred the early morning practices.*

Several usually refers to *more than a few,* but not many more than that (for example, from four to seven).
> *I chose **several** books from the library.*

Coarse/Course

Coarse is an adjective meaning *crude* or *rough.*
> *He used **coarse** language when he mistakenly applied **coarse** sandpaper to the furniture.*

Course is a noun meaning *direction taken,* or *series of studies.*
> *The canoeists had to switch **course** midstream to pass the training **course**.*

Disinterested/Uninterested

Disinterested refers to *having a neutral interest* or *being impersonal.*
> *The judge was **disinterested** in the lawyer's closing remarks.*

Uninterested refers to *being bored* or *not paying attention.*
> *The six-year-old was **uninterested** in the cartoon.*

Everyone/Every one

Everyone is the general expression, except when emphasis is desired; in that case, *every one* is used.
> **Everyone** *is going to the concert tonight.*

> **Every one** *of us is expected to make an individual contribution.*

Fewer/Less

Fewer refers to *things which can be counted or itemized.*
> *There were **fewer** voters than in the last election.*

Less refers to *general amounts.*
> *Toronto gets **less** snow than Halifax.*

Forth/Fourth

Forth means *forward* or *onward in time.*
> *The captain stepped **forth** to accept the responsibility for the team's play.*

> *From this day **forth**, loud noises won't be tolerated.*

Fourth refers to *that which comes after third.*
> *It was the **fourth** time he'd watched that film, which was one of his favourites.*

Funny/Strange

Funny is used as an informal term meaning *odd* or *strange*. But strictly speaking, *funny* refers to *something that is laughable or hilarious.*
> *Jim Carrey is one of the best-known **funny** men in recent movie history.*

Strange is a more limited term referring to the *unfamiliar* or *unnatural.*
> *Using crutches for the first time can be a **strange** experience.*

Good/Well

Good is an adjective.
> *Is this a **good** book to read?*

Well is an adverb.
> *You write **well**.*

Hear/Here

Hear is a verb referring to *the act of listening.*
> *Did you **hear** the sound of thunder?*

Here is used as an adverb or as a subject and means *in this place.*
> *The dog came **here** and sat down.*
>
> ***Here** are several reasons for courtesy.*

Hole/Whole

Hole refers to an *opening* or *hollow.*
> *Moths had eaten a **hole** through my favourite sweater.*

Whole means *complete,* or *entirety.*
> *I ate the **whole** bowl of popcorn!*

Imply/Infer

Imply means *suggest.*
> *Her expression **implied** that she disagreed with me.*

Infer means *draw a conclusion.*
> *I **infer** from your smile that you're happy with the result.*

It's/Its

It's is a contraction of *it is* or *it has. Its* is a pronoun like *his* or *hers.*
> *Look at the dog—**it's** got my shoe in **its** mouth.*

Later/Latter/Former

Later refers to *time.*
> *The buses were running **later** than usual.*

Latter refers to *the last-mentioned item; former* refers to *the first or previously mentioned item.*
> *Both Lester B. Pearson and Pierre Elliott Trudeau were Canadian prime ministers. The **former** served as prime minister for five years, and the **latter** for fifteen years.*

Lay/Lie

Lay can be used as a verb meaning *place an object, especially horizontally or in a specified place.*
> ***Lay** down your weapons.*

Lie can be used as a verb meaning *be in or assume a horizontal position on a surface; be at rest on something.* The past tense of *lie* is *lay.*
> *The doctor told the sick man to **lie** down.*
>
> *Last night I was so tired I **lay** down and instantly fell asleep.*

Lead/Led

Lead can be used as a verb (pronounced LEED) meaning *guide,* or as a noun (pronounced LED) meaning *a kind of metal.*

*You can **lead** the small children safely to the other side of the street.*

*Consumption of **lead** can be toxic.*

Led is the past tense of the verb *to lead.*

*She **led** the team to victory last week.*

Leave/Let

Leave is often used as a verb meaning *go away, place,* or *let remain.*

***Leave** whenever you want.*

***Leave** the cellphone on the hall table.*

***Leave** the box where it is.*

Let is a verb meaning *allow.*

*Jacob would not **let** us into the room.*

Like/As/Similar to

Like can be used as a preposition, and *as* can be used as an adverb. *Similar to* is a more formal expression of *like.*

*The two of them look **like** brothers.*

*The pony ran **as** fast **as** the wind.*

*The daughters were **similar to** their mother in height.*

Loan/Borrow

Loan can be used as a verb meaning *allow someone the use of,* or as a noun meaning *payment,* or *something borrowed.*

*The library will **loan** books and DVDs to anyone with a valid library card.*

*The bank gave us a **loan** to start our small business.*

Borrow is a verb meaning *use someone else's property or money.*

*May I **borrow** your pen?*

Lose/Loose/Loss

These three words are often mispronounced and misspelled. *Lose* (pronounced LOOZ) is a verb meaning *be defeated.*

*We have to learn how to **lose** graciously.*

Loose (pronounced LOOS) is an adjective meaning *not contained.*

*Do you have any **loose** change?*

*Don't let the alligator **loose**.*

Loss is a noun referring to a defeat.

*How did the home team take the **loss**?*

Off of/Off

Off of is an extremely informal expression for *off.* Use *off* rather than *off of* in writing.

*The fork fell **off** the table.*

OK/O.K./Okay

These are informal expressions for the more formal *all right.* Check your dictionary for the preferred spelling of this expression, and then use it consistently.

*Is it **OK** to leave early?*

Passed/Past

Passed is the past tense of the verb *pass*.
The car passed us on the highway.

Past is used as a noun, adjective, or preposition.
*Don't dwell on what happened in the **past**.*

*Her **past** life caught up with her.*

*He drove **past** the exit.*

Peace/Piece

Peace refers to *quiet*, or *a state of non-war*.
*Sophia enjoyed the **peace** she felt while feeding the ducks.*

Piece refers to *a section or portion*.
*Please give me a **piece** of that chocolate cake.*

Plain/Plane

Plain is an adjective meaning *obvious, ordinary*, or *simple*.
*It was **plain** that the man was guilty.*

*After the holiday decorations were removed, the room looked very **plain**.*

Plane is a shortened spelling for the noun *airplane*.
*The **plane** circled the airport before landing.*

Plus/&/And

Plus and *&* (ampersand) should be used only in mathematics, or in informal writing. Writers sometimes make the mistake of using *plus* at the beginning of a sentence to mean *also*.
*The wind **and** cold temperatures created hazardous driving conditions. **Also**, the highway was covered in black ice.*

Principal/Principle

Principal can be used as a noun meaning *head of a school*, or as an adjective meaning *main*.
*Ms. Brown, the **principal**, is the **principal** reason why this school is successful.*

Principle is a noun that refers to *fundamental belief*.
*Honesty is the guiding **principle** in his life.*

Proceed/Precede

Proceed means *go ahead*.
***Proceed** to the gym for the assembly.*

Precede means *come before*.
*A parade will **precede** the prime minister's arrival.*

Quiet/Quite/Quit

Quiet is an adjective meaning *still, peaceful, without noise*.
*Try to be **quiet** in the library.*

Quite is an adjective meaning *really, completely, actually*, or *positively*.
*Mary was **quite** upset by her brother's rudeness.*

Quit is a verb meaning *stop, leave*, or *resign*.
***Quit** doing that!*

*Three of the members **quit** the team.*

*Bella **quit** her job.*

Raise/Rise

Raise means *lift up.*
There was a plan to **raise** *the* Titanic.

Rise means *get up.*
Are you early to **rise** *in the morning?*

Real/Really

In formal usage, *real* is an adjective and *really* is an adverb.
What's the **real** *story on this cover-up?*

I swam **really** *well in the final.*

Regardless/Irregardless

The correct word is *regardless,* which means *in any case* or *in spite of.* There is no such word as *irregardless.*
They planned to go jogging **regardless** *of the bad weather.*

Role/Roll

Role is a noun, which refers to *a part played.*
What **role** *did he play in the movie?*

Roll is used as a verb meaning *turn over and over,* or as a noun referring to *a small, round piece of bread.*
Roll *the dice.*

Do I get a **roll** *with my soup order?*

Saw/Seen

Seen is sometimes used incorrectly in place of *saw,* as in *I seen the two movies before.* Note, though, that *seen* can be correct when used with the helping verbs *have* or *had.*
I **saw** *the two movies.*

I **had seen** *the two movies before.*

Should have/Should of

Never combine *of* with *should* to replace the contraction *should've,* which is short for the formally correct *should have.*
I **should have** *known better.*

Sight/Site/Cite

As a noun or verb, the more common *sight* refers to *something seen,* whereas the noun *site* refers to *place* or *centre.*
After falling in the mud, he was quite a **sight**.

Did you **sight** *that hawk?*

The **site** *for the new building overlooks the inlet.*

Cite is a verb meaning *indicate a reference.*
Remember to **cite** *all the sources you used to research your essay.*

Sure/Surely

Sure is an adjective meaning *certain* or *definite.*
The police were not **sure** *he was telling the truth.*

Surely is an adverb meaning *certainly* or *without fail.*
Surely *the jury will find him guilty.*

Than/Then

Than is used for comparison.
> *The young gymnast was more agile **than** her older competitors.*

Then is an adverb meaning *at that time*, or *soon afterward*.
> *She **then** came to a new understanding about herself.*

That/Which/Who

That can refer generally to *persons* or *things*.
> *The people **that** were in the elevator were trapped for hours.*

Which refers specifically to *things*.
> *The voting rights of citizens, **which** are guaranteed by law, make democracy work.*

Who refers only to *persons*.
> *She is the woman **who** had her purse stolen.*

There/Their/They're

There is an adverb meaning *at that place*.
> *Please put it over **there**.*

Their is a possessive pronoun meaning *belonging to them*.
> *We met my cousins at **their** house.*

They're is a contraction for *they are*.
> ***They're** always right.*

Through/Threw

Through is used as a preposition meaning *from one side to another, over*, or *by means of*.
> *The rock crashed **through** the window.*

> *You can always reach her **through** e-mail.*

Threw is the past tense of the verb *throw*, which means *toss* or *propel with force*.
> *The pitcher **threw** the ball to the catcher.*

Till/Until

These interchangeable words mean the same thing. *Till*, however, is more informal and shouldn't be used at the beginnings of sentences.
> *I'll remain here **till** it gets dark.*

> ***Until** it gets dark, I'll remain here.*

To/Too/Two

To is most often used as a preposition meaning *in the direction of*.
> *They went **to** the mall.*

Too is an adverb meaning *more than enough* or *also*.
> *If there aren't **too** many people signed up for the field trip, I'm going **too**.*

Two is the word for the numeral 2.
> ***Two** players were traded before the deadline.*

Use to/Used to

Use to is a mispronounced informal usage for the grammatically correct *used to*.
> *He is **used to** performing in front of large crowds.*

Waist/Waste

Waist refers to *that part of the body between the ribs and the hips.*
*Her costume required her to wear a shawl tied low at her **waist**.*

Waste is a noun meaning *discarded material* or *garbage*, or a verb meaning *make poor use of.*
*There was lots of **waste** on the streets after the parade.*

*Don't **waste** this opportunity to earn all your necessary credits.*

Wear/Where

Wear is a verb meaning *put on the body*, or a noun and verb both referring to *damage done to something.*
*What should we **wear** to our graduation?*

*The rear tires were showing signs of **wear**.*

Where is an adverb meaning *in (at/to/from) what place.*
***Where** are you going?*

Weather/Whether

Weather is a noun referring to *atmospheric conditions.*
*We watch the **weather** carefully when we're sailing.*

Whether is a conjunction suggesting *choice* and is often followed by *or not.*
*She did not know **whether or not** to make a donation to this charity.*

Which/Witch

Which is a pronoun or adjective used to ask questions.
***Which** route are you taking to get to downtown?*

*Tell me **which** you like best.*

Witch is a noun referring to *a woman supposed to have magical powers.*
*On Halloween, my sister dressed up as a **witch**.*

Who's/Whose

Who's is a contraction of *who is* or *who has.*
*Samir, **who's** planning a trip in the spring, is looking for a part-time job.*

***Who's** got the puck?*

Whose is a possessive pronoun expressing *ownership.*
***Whose** books are these?*

Would of/Would have

Would of is a misspelling of the contraction *would've*, short for the formally correct *would have.*
*We **would have** attended the concert if we had known how good it was going to be.*

You're/Your

You're is a contraction for *you are.*
***You're** just the person to do that job.*

Your is a possessive pronoun meaning *belonging to you.*
***Your** grades are improving.*

Spelling

The ability to spell correctly is like any other writing skill: it takes commitment and practice. In the sections that follow, you will find basic spelling rules, hints for solving problems with spelling, and a list of commonly misspelled words.

Basic Spelling Rules

The basic spelling rules that follow are well worth knowing.

To change singular nouns to plural:
- add *s*: *bird* → *birds*

- for nouns ending in *s*, add *es*: *bus* → *buses*

- for nouns ending in *y*, drop the *y* and add *ies*: *family* → *families*

Never use an apostrophe followed by an *s* (*'s*) to indicate a plural noun.

five friends came, not *five friend's came*

If, however, a plural noun ending in *s* shows possession, add an apostrophe after the *s* (*s'*):

my two friends' choices

Use *i* before *e* except after *c*.

sieve, brief, relieve, yield, friend

receive, deceit, receipt, ceiling

Exceptions include *ei* when it makes a long vowel *a* sound.

neighbour, weigh, vein, freight, sleigh

Other exceptions simply need to be memorized:

being, foreign, leisure, their, either, seize, weird

Double the end consonant (such as *n*, *p*, or *t*) before adding *-ed* or *-ing* suffixes when the end consonant is preceded by a short vowel sound.

beginning, shopped, occurring, permitted

Drop the *e* before *-able* suffixes.

value → *valuable, excite* → *excitable, love* → *lovable*

Here are some exceptions to remember:

noticeable, knowledgeable, changeable

Soft *c* and soft *g* are followed by either *e* or *i* (the reason for the exceptions when adding *-able* suffixes). Otherwise, *c* and *g* both use the hard sound.

circle, necessary, vegetable, garage

The sound *full* at the end of a word is spelled with only one *l*.

grateful, skilful, careful, hopeful

Only three verbs in English end in *-ceed: succeed, proceed,* and *exceed.* All the other verbs with that sound end in *-cede.*

precede, intercede, accede

Some words have silent letters.

pneumonia, knight, subtle, autumn, column, palm

Spelling Tips

Divide words into syllables. Make sure each syllable contains one vowel sound.

con•cern•ing, dif•fer•ent, hand•ker•chief, in•ter•est, mo•ti•va•tion

Mentally set off prefixes and suffixes from the rest of the word.

notice•able, tran•scribe, help•ful, permiss•ible, pre•view, hope•less, dis•appoint

Use memory cues based on "buried words" within longer words.

business, separate, temperature

Another memory aid is to purposely mispronounce the word by saying any silent letters or otherwise making it sound strange or funny.

knife, know, ghost, gnome

Make a list of commonly misspelled words from previous assignments.

In a notebook, make a list of words you frequently misspell in your writing. Refer to this list when proofreading new assignments.

As you are writing, underline any words you aren't sure of and then return later at the proofreading stage to check them.

When proofreading, it often helps to hold a ruler or piece of white paper under each line of text as you read to check for errors.

Use a spell-checker.

All word-processing programs come with a spell-check function. Be certain to look back over your assignment to correct the identified errors. However, be aware that there are many errors a spell-checker will not catch. For example, if you use the word *waist* when you really mean *waste*, the spell-checker will not identify the mistake.

Use a dictionary.

If uncertain about a spelling, check in a dictionary. Always check homophones, which are words that sound the same but have different spellings and meanings (for example, *its* and *it's*; *they're, there,* and *their; you're* and *your*). Pay particular attention to those homophones you know from past experience have given you trouble.

Check for frequently misspelled words.

Following is a list of commonly misspelled English words. Have a friend or family member dictate these words to you, a few at a time. Check the list for those that give you trouble.

Frequently Misspelled Words

Here is a list of words that are frequently misspelled. Are there any words here that cause you problems? If so, you might want to make a separate list of these words. Alternative spellings are also provided for certain words, but always use a preferred form consistently in the same piece of writing.

absence	athletics	column	entrepreneur
absorption	atmosphere	commitment	environment
acceptable	attendance	committee	especially
accessory	author	compatible	eventually
accidentally	autumn	completely	exaggerate
accommodation	available	concede	exceed
accompanying	barely	condemn	excellence
accumulate	basically	conscience	exercise
achieve	beginning	conscientious	exhaust
acknowledgment	behaviour	conscious	existence
or acknowledgement	or behavior	consensus	experience
acquaintance	believe	contradiction	extraordinary
acquire	benefit	convenience	extremely
actually	biassed	correspondent	fallacy
address	or biased	courageous	familiar
adjacent	boundary	courtesy	fascinating
adolescence	breathe	cried	February
advantageous	brilliant	criticism	fiery
advertisement	brochure	curiosity	finally
adviser	business	debt	flexible
or advisor	calendar	decision	foreign
advisory	campaign	definitely	foresee
affiliated	catalogue	describe	foreshadowing
aggressive	or catalog	desirable	fortunate
alleged	category	desperately	forty
all right	cemetery	destroy	fulfil
amateur	certain	develop	or fulfill
among	changeable	development	gauge
analyse	character	different	gesture
or analyze	cheque	dilemma	goddess
analysis	or check	disappointed	government
answered	chief	disastrous	grammar
anxious	chronological	discipline	grateful
apologize	clothes	doesn't	guarantee
apparent	coincidence	dying	or guaranty
appearance	collage	eighth	handkerchief
appropriate	collectible	eligible	harassment
argument	or collectable	eliminate	heroes
article	college	embarrassed	height
assistance	colonel	emphasize	

honourable
or honorable
humorous
ignorance
illegible
immediately
incidentally
incredible
independent
indispensable
inevitable
innuendo
insistent
instalment
or installment
intelligent
interesting
interfere
irrelevant
irresistible
jealous
jeopardy
jewellery
or jewelry
judgment
or judgement
knowledgeable
laid
leisure
liaison
liar
library
lightning
likable
or likeable
literature
loneliness
losing
maintenance
marriage
married
meant
mediocre
memento
miniature
minuscule
miscellaneous
mischievous
misspell

mortgage
muscle
naive
necessary
neighbour
or neighbor
niece
ninety
ninth
no one
or no-one
noticeable
nowadays
nuclear
occasionally
occurrence
offence
or offense
omission
opinion
optimistic
paid
parallel
paralyse
or paralyze
parliament
particular
pastime
peculiar
perseverance
persistence
personal
personnel
persuade
phenomenal
piece
plagiarism
playwright
portrays
possession
preceding
preferable
preferred
prejudice
presence
presumptuous
pretence
or pretense
previously

privilege
probably
procedure
proceed
professional
pronunciation
psychology
publicly
pursue
questionnaire
realistically
realize
receipt
receive
recommend
referee
referring
reinforce
related
relevant
remembrance
resemblance
restaurant
rhyme
rhythm
Saskatchewan
schedule
scheme
science
scissors
seize
sense
separate
sergeant
Shakespeare
similar
sincerely
skilful
or skillful
soldier
soliloquy
souvenir
spirited
stealth
stereotype
straight
strength
subconscious
subtle

succeed
summary
supposed
surprise
suspense
technique
temperamental
temperature
tempt
tendency
theatre
or theater
theory
therefore
thoroughly
threshold
together
tomorrow
tragedy
tragic
transferred
traveller
or traveler
tries
truly
Tuesday
twelfth
ultimately
unconscious
undoubtedly
unfortunately
unique
unnecessary
until
usage
usually
vacuum
vegetable
vehicle
vicious
view
villain
Wednesday
weird
wherever
whole
writer
writing
yield

Punctuation

In spoken English, you can use different tones of voice, pauses, and volume changes to make your meaning clear. In writing, your only tool is punctuation, so using it correctly is essential.

Apostrophe

Apostrophes (') are used for two main functions:

1. in contractions, to indicate missing letters:

   you're → *You* **are my** *closest friend.* → **You're** *my closest friend.*

   doesn't → *She* **does not** *know the correct answer.* → *She* **doesn't** *know the correct answer.*

   should've → *I* **should have** *listened to you.* → *I* **should've** *listened to you.*

2. in possessives, to indicate ownership:

   the shirt that belongs to John → *John's shirt*

- A single owner is written as *'s*, while plural owners are indicated by *s'*.

   Hannah's skateboard (one Hannah), *my dog's toys* (one dog)

   the Smiths' house (more than one Smith), *my dogs' toys* (more than one dog)

- Some writers prefer to write *s's* for the possessive of names ending in *s*.

   Charles Dickens's story (pronounced *Dickenzez*) although *Dickens' story* is also correct.

   James's team can also be written as *James' team*.

- How can you be sure that a possessive apostrophe is required? There will be two nouns side by side.

   Sanjit's car, my sister's bike, the teacher's comments

- Some words form irregular plurals that do not end in *s*. Therefore, you do not add *s'* to these:

   men's shoes, women's clothing, children's toys

- Never use an apostrophe with *his, hers, theirs, yours,* or *ours*.

One common mistake is to assume that every word ending in *s* needs an apostrophe, even if the word is not a contraction or is not being used as a possessive. The following is *incorrect*:

The concert's were both well staged.

Look carefully and ask yourself if letters are missing. Ask yourself what belongs to the concert, and you will see that the answer is *nothing*. The apostrophe is therefore not needed.

Another common mistake is to use *it's* instead of *its*, and vice versa. The contraction is *it's* (*it is* or *it has*) and always has an apostrophe.

It's a nice day. (It is a nice day.)

The possessive is *its* (*belonging to it*) and never has an apostrophe.

The dog has chewed its basket.

Colon

Colons (:) are used in three common ways:

1. Before a list:

   We added the following ingredients: flour, eggs, and milk.

2. Before an explanation, illustration, or restatement of a point or idea. The colon tells us there is more to come:

   The author made his point very clearly: people cannot be trusted.

3. Before a long quotation, such as a passage quoted from a book.

Commas (,) are used in several ways:

- To punctuate items in a series:

  Jacob, Maris, and Tomas are flying to Toronto.

  They will have less than an hour to arrive at the check-in, clear customs, check their bags, and board their plane.

  The comma before the next-to-last item is optional, but it is necessary when two items are treated as a unit, as with *Mei Lin and Tom* in the following example. Here, three presentations are being given, not four.

  John, Mei Lin and Tom, and Susan will give their presentations tomorrow.

- To set off a transitional word, phrase, or clause at the beginning of a sentence:

  Clearly, that team gave us no difficulty.

  In the end, we had the better players.

  When all is said and done, my best times are spent with my friends.

- To set off additional or supportive information from the rest of the sentence. This information is called an appositive.

  My employer, Mr. Santini, wants me to work an extra hour on Saturday.

  I finally came home to my best friend, my dog.

- To set off words or phrases that qualify the meaning of a sentence. Such commas always work in pairs, unless the qualification comes at the beginning or end of the sentence.

  The spectators rose and cheered when, after what seemed like forever, our team finally scored.

  However, we tried to do the best job possible.

  We tried to do the best job possible, however.

  Sometimes referred to as parenthetical information, the qualifying words or phrases could be removed from the sentence, leaving behind a complete, grammatically correct sentence.

- Before a conjunction that links the two parts of a compound sentence, especially when the sentence is lengthy or the information in the second clause conflicts with or contradicts information in the first:

    It was their visit to the dense forest that covered the slopes of the highest mountain on the island, and they were dazzled by the greenness of the vegetation.

    The Cougars lost the first game, but they eventually won the series.

- Following someone's name when you are addressing that person:

    Dad, come here quickly!

- Separating items in addresses or dates:

    He lives at 851 Atlantic Drive, Truro, Nova Scotia.

    I was born on Wednesday, October 24, 1991.

- Preceding direct speech:

    She replied, "This will be my first time on an airplane."

- Sometimes, commas need to be used to clarify otherwise confusing information:

    After I ate my pet turtle disappeared.

    Obviously, a comma after *ate* would help to clarify what actually happened.

    After I ate, my pet turtle disappeared.

As a general rule, it's best not to use a comma unless you know why you are using it. If you are in doubt, omit the comma.

Dash

Dashes (—) are used to separate sidetracking or contrasting parenthetical information from the rest of the sentence.

The piece of metal—which everyone had completely forgotten about—got stuck in the gearshift.

The dash indicates a strong, emphatic break in the sentence.

Ellipsis Points

Ellipsis points (...) are used to indicate that words have been omitted from a statement.

He promised that he would complete the manuscript and turn it in to the publisher on time. (original statement)

He promised that he would complete the manuscript ... on time. (showing omitted words)

If the omitted words come at the end of a statement, then add a fourth point—the period.

He promised that he would complete the manuscript....

End Punctuation

A sentence ends with a period, a question mark, or an exclamation mark.

- Use a period at the end of a statement (declarative sentence).

  I have to catch the bus.

- If the sentence is a question, use a question mark. This is called an interrogative sentence.

  Why do you have to catch that bus?

- In some statements, you may want to convey urgency or strong emotion. Use an exclamation mark.

  I must catch that bus!

- As a rule, only one end punctuation mark is used in formal and in most creative writing. Do not use punctuation in a distracting manner, as the following example does:

  You made me miss the bus!!!

  Only one exclamation mark is needed for the required emphasis:

  You made me miss the bus!

Hyphen

Hyphens (-) are used mainly as follows:

- in some compound words

  fail-safe, short-circuit, half-hearted

- to link connected words

  easy-to-use, paint-by-number

- between numbers

  twenty-nine, four-sevenths

- with some prefixes

  anti-inflation, ex-student, semi-intelligent, de-ice

Parentheses

Parentheses ( ) are used to add extra information (referred to as parenthetical information) in order to elaborate or make something more clear.

> *Mike was afraid of dogs. (As a child he had been bitten at a dog show.)*

This effect should be used sparingly in an essay to avoid an unpolished appearance.

Quotation Marks

- Quotation marks (" ") are mainly used to indicate the words someone has said.

  "We need more punctuation practice," Cordell said.

- Single quotation marks are used to indicate a quotation within a quotation.

  Jessica asked, "Did Cordell just say, 'We need more punctuation practice'?"

- Commas and periods are always placed inside the end quotation mark.

  Prem answered, "I already have too much homework."

- Question marks and exclamation marks go inside the end quotation mark when the quoted material is a question or an exclamation.

  Sean yelled in frustration, "Give it to me—it's mine!"

- Question marks and exclamation marks go outside the end quotation mark when the whole sentence is a question or exclamation, but the quoted part is not.

  Did you hear Meagan say, "I found that book"?

- The titles of brief works of literature (songs, poems, short stories, newspaper or magazine articles, and essays) are set in quotation marks. Such titles are not italicized.

  "Somewhere Over the Rainbow" (song title)

  "The Road Not Taken" (poem title)

Semicolon

- Semicolons (;) create separation between two independent clauses that are closely related, but are not separated by a conjunction such as *and* or *but*.

  Moira knew her limitations; she knew when to quit.

- In a single sentence, when the two clauses are joined by a transitional word such as *however, also,* or *consequently,* the linking word is preceded by a semicolon or a period and followed by a comma.

  I know the answer; however, I may just keep it to myself.

  The two sentences can also be written separately.

  I know the answer. However, I may just keep it to myself.

- When items in a series have more than one part to each item, use semicolons to clarify the main items.

  Special airfares were available for Halifax, the capital of Nova Scotia; Toronto, the capital of Ontario; and Winnipeg, the capital of Manitoba.

Square Brackets

Square brackets [ ] are used to set off words that do not appear in an original quotation but that help to clarify meaning. They should be used sparingly.

  He asked, "Is there anyone [of those invited] still to come?"

  Punctuation marks are the traffic signals of language.

  Lynne Truss

Capitalization

Capitals are required for:

- the first letter of the first word at the beginning of a sentence
- the first letter of the first word of a quotation

  She asked me, "When did you get here?"

- the first letter of a language, nationality, ethnic group, or religion
- the first letter of a family-relationship word used as a name

  I call my mother Mom.

- the first letter of all important words in proper nouns, including names of persons, personal titles, brand names, business firms, and organizations
- the first letter of all important words in the names of holidays and historical events

  Canada Day, the Great War

- the first letter of all important words in the names of publications

  The Daily News, Seventeen, The Hockey Digest, Car and Driver

- the first letter of all important words in the titles of books, short stories, poems, movies, and songs

  Nelson Canadian Writer's Handbook
  "The Pit and the Pendulum"
  "We Are the Champions"

HERMAN®   by Jim Unger

4-20   © Jim Unger/dist. by United Media, 2000

The capital of Holland is 'H'.

Titles

Here are some basic rules to remember when quoting titles within your writing:

- Use quotation marks to identify shorter works such as short stories, poems, essays, newspaper or magazine articles, and songs. Do not use italics.

  "What Language Do Bears Speak?"

  "Raging snowstorm batters Montréal"

- Use italics (or underlining when writing by hand) for longer works. This includes names of newspapers and magazines, books, television series, and feature films.

  The Globe and Mail (newspaper)

  Maclean's (magazine)

  Harry Potter and the Deathly Hallows (book)

Writing Numbers

Styles vary, but usually the following hold true:

- Numbers from one to ten are written out in full.

  five, nine

- Numbers from 11 up are represented by numerals.

  100, 2001

- Fractions are generally written in full. Exceptions may include reports written in math or science.

  one-half

- Numbers written as adjectives or adverbs are generally written in full.

  first, nineteenth

Appendix

Note Taking

Note taking is a key skill for learning. Essentially, it helps you learn in two ways:

- You record and remember information you've read, heard, or seen.

- You make this information your own as you summarize and highlight important points.

Skilful note taking is an active process that helps you focus on important information so that you can make sense of it.

Here are some guidelines for developing your note-taking skills:

- Block out distractions and pay close attention to the source of the information. If you're reading something, find a quiet spot where you can concentrate on the material. If your source is a speaker or a recording, listen carefully. If it's a visual source, such as a photograph, look closely at the different parts of the image.

- Write legibly, even if you're writing quickly. You must be able to read your own notes.

- Make sure you understand your purpose in taking the notes. For example, are they to help you identify possible ideas to include in an opinion piece or to summarize information for use in an oral presentation?

- Do not try to note down everything. Write in point form, making it clear which are major points and which are minor. Record—and underline, circle, or star—any key words and phrases used.

- Look out or listen for words and phrases such as *main, key, most important, in the first place, remember, necessary,* and *urgent.* They signal that an important point is being made. If you're listening to a speaker, pay attention to significant pauses or emphases and to information presented in visual aids such as flipcharts, overhead projections, and PowerPoint slides.

- Note important specific examples and details such as names, statistics, quotations, or page-number references.

- Use abbreviations or symbols, even ones you invent yourself, such as:

  + or & for *and*   b/c for *because*   bk for *book*   gov for *government*

  = for *same as*   w/o for *without*   impt. or ! for *important*

- Note questions or points that you want to pursue (for example, a question to ask the teacher or presenter or a point that needs further research).

- Use a graphic organizer, such as one of the examples suggested on the following page, to help you organize your notes.

- Review your notes within 24 hours to make sure you understand them. Fill in any important information that you were unable to record while it's still fresh in your mind.

A simple and effective system of note taking is to divide your notes page into two columns, like the sample below. On the left side, write each of the main ideas being presented. On the right side, write (in point form) the important details or examples for that same idea or paragraph/section, or list your own thoughts, questions, or observations about the ideas.

This two-column method can be very helpful when you're reviewing material. Fold the page to cover the examples and specific details in the right column; what you'll see on the left is a handy overview of the main ideas.

MAIN IDEA	EXAMPLES AND SPECIFIC DETAILS
Romeo acts without thinking	• tries to make peace between Mercutio and Tybalt—causes friend's death • rushes to Juliet's tomb before Friar Lawrence's letter arrives • kills himself without checking to see if she's alive

Another approach to note taking is to use visual organizers such as flowcharts, time lines, webs, and T-charts (for examples, see pages 34–35). These help you to show graphically how different pieces of information are linked (for instance, a sequence of events, causes and their effects, problems and their possible solutions, and the similarities and differences between two things or people). A Venn diagram, like the one below comparing two people, is especially useful for the last example. Similarities are placed in the overlapping middle section of the diagram and differences in the separate parts of the circles.

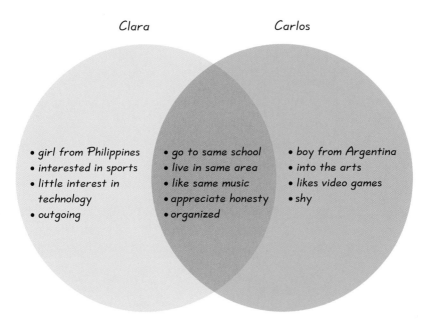

Clara

Carlos

- girl from Philippines
- interested in sports
- little interest in technology
- outgoing

- go to same school
- live in same area
- like same music
- appreciate honesty
- organized

- boy from Argentina
- into the arts
- likes video games
- shy

Managing Your Time

Here are some tips to help you keep track of your schoolwork and manage your time more efficiently:

- Use a planner or calendar to note down assignment due dates, as well as times for recreational and other personal activities. Get in the habit of looking at it several times every day and updating it as required. This will help you to meet deadlines, keep appointments, and stay on top of your social life. Below is a sample from a student's daily planner:

Monday	October 20, 2008
11 a.m.	Study period—prepare for English project discussion tomorrow
noon	Lunch with Jess and Ali!
1 p.m.	History presentation—reread Chapter 3, esp. time line on page 65
2 p.m.	Learning Resource Centre—look for resources for science project

- Once a week, allow some time for short-term planning of what you need to do over the next week. Once a month, allow time for long-term planning, organizing what you need to do over the coming two to four months. Set priorities by highlighting important dates, work, or goals. Below is a sample of a calendar showing an overview of activities for a week.

Monday, October 20
Science project due next Monday

Tuesday, October 21
Meet with group to discuss English project

Wednesday, October 22
Study for French quiz

Thursday, October 23
French quiz

Friday, October 24
Final band rehearsal

Saturday, October 25
School concert

Sunday, October 26
Larry arriving from Ottawa

- Use the amount of time you're given to complete an assignment as a clue to what's expected. If you're assigned a writing project today that is due in two days, chances are you won't be expected to do a lot of research or write anything lengthy. You will, however, be expected to present ideas that are well thought out, clearly written, and carefully proofread. On the other hand, if you have a week or more to complete the assignment, you can budget more time for research or preparation, start the assignment early, be prepared to develop your ideas in more detail, and spend time revising your writing. Whatever the assignment, make sure you understand exactly what's expected, and by when.

- Break down big assignments into smaller tasks, and estimate the amount of time you will need for each task. For example, if you're writing a research paper, you will probably need to set aside about half the time you have available for the actual research. The other half can be divided among drafting, revising, editing, proofreading, and publishing a final copy.

- Set aside particular times for completing an assignment, and stick to your schedule. A regular routine will help you to concentrate when it's time to work, as well as to relax when it isn't.

- Always leave enough time for eating, sleeping, exercising, socializing with friends and family, and just being by yourself.

- Cut down on distractions. This might include watching less television, playing fewer video games, talking on the phone less frequently, text messaging less, and spending less time checking and answering e-mail.

- Be assertive about managing your time. Politely tell others that you are busy because you have work to do or have other, more pressing priorities.

- Get (and stay) organized. With some practice and self-discipline, managing your time successfully will become a routine part of your life.

Glossary

Abbreviation

An abbreviation is a shortened form of a word or phrase. There is a trend away from using periods in abbreviations, especially for companies or organizations (e.g., *RCMP*). In most instances, abbreviations are not used in formal writing. A few exceptions include the following:

- titles such as *Ms., Mr., Dr.*
- *St.* for *Saint* in some place names
- degrees or professional titles, such as *B.A., Ph.D., LL.B., M.B.A.*, when placed after a person's name
- indications of time when used with figures, such as *7 p.m.*

Acronym

An acronym is an abbreviation that forms an artificial word based on the first letter or first few letters of a group of words, for example:

NATO North Atlantic Treaty Organization

SWAT Special Weapons and Tactics (team)

sonar sound navigation and ranging

Adjective

An adjective (word, phrase, or clause) is used for the following:

- to modify a noun: *We heard a <u>loud</u> noise. His <u>icy blue</u> eyes stared at nothing.*
- to modify a pronoun: *<u>Poor</u> me! She looked <u>pale</u>.*
- to answer the question *what kind?* (*<u>sunny</u> weather*), *how many?* (*<u>seven</u> days*), or *which one?* (*the <u>biggest</u> book*)

Adjectives either precede the noun they describe, or follow a linking verb and describe the subject of the sentence. Example: *The cat is <u>hungry</u>.*

An *indefinite adjective* indicates an unspecified person or thing: *another, each, much, any, some, such.* Example: *Each person must be present.* (*Each* modifies *person.*) Note that these words can also act as pronouns. Example: *Each must be present.* (*Each* is the subject of the sentence.)

Adverb

An adverb (word, phrase, or clause) is used for the following:

- to modify a verb: *He left the party <u>early</u>.*
- to modify an adjective: *Her face was <u>slightly</u> sunburned.*
- to modify another adverb: *We left the party <u>very</u> early.*
- to answer the question *how?* (*I spoke <u>softly</u>*), *when?* (*I arrived <u>late</u>*), or *where?* (*Move the chair <u>forward</u>*)

All words ending in *–ly* (except for nouns such as *family, lily*) are adverbs.

Agreement

SEE **Pronoun Usage** and **Subject-Verb Agreement**

Allusion

An allusion is a casual or passing reference to a historical, religious, mythological, or pop-culture person, place, or event, or to another literary or artistic work or character assumed to be familiar to the reader.

She seems to have adopted a Barbie-like fashion style.

If it rains much longer, I'm going to start building an ark.

SEE also **Figurative Language/Figure of Speech**

Antecedent

An antecedent is a noun or a noun phrase to which a following pronoun refers. The noun or noun phrase and its antecedent may occur in the same sentence or in separate sentences.

John was new to the class and I thought he seemed more mature than the others.
(*John* is the antecedent of *he*.)

I met Miriam at the rink. While skating one evening, I felt the laces on one skate to be too tight. I glided over to the bench by the gate to sit down and saw her standing there.
(*Miriam* is the antecedent of *her* in the third sentence.)

Antonym

Antonyms are words that mean the opposite of each other. For example, antonyms for the verb *hate* include *like, admire, enjoy, love,* and *adore*.

SEE also **Synonym**

Appositive

SEE **Noun**

Article

The *definite article* (*the*) indicates that the noun that follows the indefinite article refers to something or someone in particular: *the book*. The *indefinite articles* (*a* and *an*) indicate that the noun that follows the indefinite article belongs to a particular category: *a book of fiction*.

Atmosphere

Atmosphere is the emotional tone in a piece of writing or media text, created through the skilful use of words, images, dialogue, description, and/or narration.

SEE also **Mood**

Balance

Balance is the quality of writing in which items or passages are given similar treatment or weight. A balanced construction features two parts, each of about the same importance and length. Items that may be balanced include words or phrases in a sentence, sentences in a paragraph, or paragraphs in a longer passage. Example: *It was the biggest game of our season, and the greatest letdown of our lives.*

SEE also **Parallel Structure**

Bibliography

A bibliography (sometimes called *Works Cited* or *References*) is a list of all the works cited in an essay or research paper, placed on one or more pages at the end of the paper. All bibliographies include the same basic information arranged alphabetically by the name of the author(s), followed by the title of the work, the name of the publisher, and the place and date of publication. Example: Truss, Lynne. *Eats, Shoots & Leaves.* New York: Gotham Books, 2006.

SEE also **Citation**

Block Quotation

A block quotation is a long quotation that is separated from the body of a research paper and indented from the left margin. No quotation marks are needed because the indent signals that the copy is quoted material.

Citation

Citations are used in an essay or research paper to acknowledge the sources of quotations, charts, tables, diagrams, and all ideas other than your own.

SEE also **Bibliography**, **Endnotes**, and **Footnotes**

Clause

A clause is a group of related words with a subject and a verb.

- A *principal clause* (also known as an *independent* or *main clause*) expresses a complete thought and can stand alone as a sentence. Example: *The trip downtown bored me.*
- A *subordinate clause* (also known as a *dependent clause*) does not express a complete thought and cannot stand alone as a sentence. Example: <u>*Until we reached Chinatown*</u>, *the trip downtown bored me.*

SEE also **Phrase** and **Sentence**

Cliché

A cliché is an overworked expression that has lost its effectiveness. Its use suggests lazy writing and is best avoided. Examples: *free as a bird, a total team effort, what goes around comes around, no pain no gain, last but not least*

Coherence

Coherence is a quality of writing in which the parts relate to each other clearly and logically. Coherence is considered a principle of effective writing.

SEE also **Transitional Devices** and **Transition Sentence**

Colloquialism

A colloquialism is an expression that is used in informal spoken or written language, but not in formal speech or writing. Colloquial expressions give writing a conversational tone, making it more informal and often more entertaining than formal writing. Examples: *tough break, no way, sweet*

SEE also **Formal/Informal Language**

Comma Splice

A comma splice is an error in comma use, in which two simple sentences have been joined in an attempt to form a compound sentence by means of a comma alone. Example: *She fixed the computer, now it could be used.*

SEE also **Run-on Sentence** and **Sentence**

Compare/Contrast

Comparison and contrast are techniques for examining two or more items or topics to highlight their similarities and/or differences. Comparisons emphasize similarities; contrasts emphasize differences.

Compound Word

A compound word is a combination of two or more words that forms a new word with its own meaning. Some compound words are written as one word (*hotline*), some are hyphenated (*hang-gliding*), and some are written as separate words (*check mark*). Check your dictionary for its preferred forms of compound words.

Conjunction

A conjunction is a word that connects words, phrases, or clauses, and indicates the relationship between them.

- A *co-ordinating conjunction* connects two words, phrases, or clauses of equal rank. There are seven of them: *and, but, or, nor, for, yet,* and *so.* Example: *I would like to go to the concert, <u>but</u> I have no money.*
- A *correlative conjunction* connects two words, phrases, or clauses of equal rank, but this type of conjunction is used in pairs, such as *both ... and; not only ... but also; either ... or;* and *neither ... nor.* Example: <u>*Either*</u> *we do this right, <u>or</u> we don't do it at all.*

- A *subordinating conjunction* connects a subordinate clause to a principal, or independent, clause. Common subordinating conjunctions include *after, although, because, before, if, since, unless, when,* and *while.* Example: *I break out in hives <u>whenever</u> I eat pickles.*

Connective

A connective is a word that joins words, phrases, or clauses. Connectives are usually conjunctions (*and, or*), prepositions (*near, around*), and relative pronouns (*who, which*). Transitional devices are also connectives (*however, for example*).

Connotation/Denotation

Connotation and denotation are two categories or levels of word meaning. The denotation of a word is its basic, literal dictionary meaning. The connotation of a word refers to an additional level of meaning or overtone and the emotions or associations aroused by the word.

Denotation of the word *home: The place where a person, family, or creature lives permanently.*

Connotations of the word *home: safety, comfort, family, rest, belonging*

Words are often understood to carry positive or negative connotations. For example, *slender* has a positive connotation, while *scrawny* has a negative connotation.

SEE also **Synonym** and **Tone**

Context

Context is the personal, social, or historical circumstance or background that a writer needs to establish if a reader is to appreciate fully the significance of a work. For example, the context of World War II and the Holocaust may be necessary to understand a story set in Europe in the 1940s.

Contraction

A contraction is a shortening of two words into one, in which an apostrophe shows where letters have been omitted: *doesn't = does not; I've = I have; there's = there is* or *there has.*

SEE also **Formal/Informal Language**

Conventions

The conventions of written language are the accepted practices used to help convey meaning. There are conventions for spelling, punctuation, grammar, usage, and capitalization. There are also conventions related to the presentation of a piece of writing, for elements such as illustrations, charts, headings and subheadings, the table of contents, and so on.

Critical Response

A critical response is a serious examination of a topic or literary work, with as little reference as possible to personal views, biasses, values, or beliefs. A critical response is written in the third person and aims to be objective and neutral in its presentation of ideas and supporting evidence.

SEE also **Personal Response**

Denotation

SEE **Connotation/Denotation**

Description/Descriptive Writing

Description is writing in which the author's purpose is to use words to create a mental picture that stimulates an emotional response in the reader.

Dialogue

SEE **Script**

Diction

Diction refers to the writer's choice and use of words to express ideas in either spoken or written language.

Double Negative

Using two negative words (such as *not* and *never*) in the same sentence results in a double negative. Example: *He doesn't have none!* Avoid confusion by removing or replacing one of the two negative words. Double negatives often occur in sentences in which the word *not* is hidden in a contraction, such as *can't*. Example: *They can't never get that straight.*

Emphasis

Emphasis is the stressing of or calling attention to important ideas in a sentence, paragraph, or longer piece of writing. Emphasis can be achieved through the specific positioning of an idea (usually near the beginning or the end of a sentence, paragraph, or longer piece of writing), as well as through repetition, parallelism, elaboration, or italicization.

Endnotes

Endnotes are used to acknowledge the sources of quotations, charts, tables, diagrams, and all ideas other than your own; they appear at the end of a piece of writing such as an essay or research paper, and are identified by superscript numbers.

SEE also **Citations** and **Footnotes**

Euphemism

A euphemism is a word or expression that is meant to avoid the use of words or phrases with unpleasant or offensive associations. Some common euphemisms are *pass away* for *die* and *pre-owned* for *used*. As shown by the military use of terms such as *collateral damage* instead of *deaths*, there can be a fine line between using a euphemism and obscuring the truth.

Exclamation Mark [!]

An exclamation mark at the end of a sentence or phrase gives emphasis and expresses surprise, delight, or alarm. Example: *Watch out!* Most writers trust their words to express whatever mood or emotion they wish to convey. When used sparingly, exclamation marks can be helpful, but too many may weaken their effect.

Exposition/Expository Writing

Exposition is writing in which the author's purpose is to explain something, such as how to manage your time or how to operate a machine.

Figurative Language/Figures of Speech

Figurative language (also called figures of speech) refers to words used in ways that go beyond their literal dictionary meanings to enhance their impact on the reader. Example: *It's raining cats and dogs.* Similes and metaphors are two of the most common figures of speech.

SEE also **Similes**, **Metaphors**, **Hyperbole**, and **Personification**

Flashback

Flashback is a technique often used in writing or in a media text to interrupt the sequence of events of a narrative by going back to an earlier event.

Footnotes

Footnotes are used in an essay or research paper to acknowledge the sources of quotations, charts, tables, diagrams, and all ideas other than your own. They appear at the bottom of the same page in which the citation, identified by a superscript number, occurs.

SEE also **Citations** and **Endnotes**

Formal/Informal Language

- *Formal language* is language that follows the rules of grammar, spelling, punctuation, and capitalization. It often contains comparatively sophisticated words, and is used in most school writing assignments, textbooks, technical writing, and speeches. It generally avoids first-person pronouns (*I, me, mine, my*) and contractions.

- *Informal language* is the language of everyday conversation. It is also used in informal writing such as e-mails, letters to friends and relatives, advertising, magazines of general interest, personal narratives, and personal essays. Informal style allows the use of contractions, colloquialisms, and first-person pronouns.

SEE also **Contraction, Colloquialism, Idiom,** and **Slang**

Fused Sentence

SEE **Run-on Sentence**

Genre

Genre refers to a kind or type of literary work. For example, poetry is a genre of literature. Poetry can be further subdivided into specific subgenres, including ballad, lyric, and sonnet.

Homonym/Homophone

- *Homonyms* are words that are pronounced the same but have different meanings. They may also be spelled the same, such as *ear* (organ for hearing) and *ear* (of corn).

- *Homophones* are words that are pronounced the same but have different meanings and spellings, such as *see* and *sea*.

Hyperbole

Hyperbole is a figure of speech in which extreme exaggeration is used for emphatic effect. Example: *I wouldn't go to that movie if you gave me a million dollars.*

SEE also **Figurative Language/Figures of Speech**

Idiom

An idiom is a colourful word, phrase, or expression that is used and easily understood by people who speak the same language. Some examples in English are *to catch a cold, to be a pain in the neck, to take after one's mother,* and *how do you do?* These combinations often seem odd or puzzling to people who are not completely fluent in the language in which the idiom is used, because the meaning of the idiom is different from the literal meaning of the words.

SEE also **Formal/Informal Language**

Imagery

Imagery is the use of language to create vivid pictures in the mind of a reader or listener by appealing to the senses of sight, sound, smell, taste, and touch.

SEE also **Description/Descriptive Writing**

Interjection

An interjection is a word that expresses emotion, and is often followed by an exclamation mark: <u>Oh</u>, *you scared me!* Some other interjections are *ah, hello, hey, oops, ouch, no,* and *yes.*

Interrogatives

Interrogatives are the words used in asking questions.

- Interrogative adverbs are *where, when, why, how,* and their compounds (for example, *wherever*).
- Interrogative pronouns are *who, which, what,* and their compounds (for example, *whoever*).

Irony

Irony occurs when what is meant is the opposite of what is actually expressed, such as a student who has just failed a test referring to herself as "a genius." Ironic situations are those in which the opposite of what might be expected actually occurs, such as an environmental activist driving an SUV.

Jargon

Jargon is the formal, specialized language of a particular group or profession. When used in writing intended for a wide audience, such words should be explained (for example, legal or medical terms). Most writers try to avoid using jargon.

SEE also **Formal/Informal Language**

Linking Words and Phrases

SEE **Transitional Devices**

Metaphor

A metaphor makes a comparison implicitly between two things, without using *like* or *as.* Example: *Bony fingers of ice hung from the edge of the roof.*

SEE also **Figurative Language/Figures of Speech** and **Simile**

Modifier

A modifier is a word, phrase, or clause that qualifies the meaning of a word.

- A *misplaced modifier* appears to modify the wrong word or words because it is positioned too far from what it modifies. For example, *She watched the sun rise from her balcony* has a misplaced modifier. This sentence seems to say that the sun was rising from the balcony. A clearer sentence would be *From her balcony, she watched the sun rise.*
- A *dangling modifier* occurs when the word being modified does not appear in the sentence. *While on holiday, a thief broke into our house* seems to say that the thief was on holiday. A better sentence would be *While we were on holiday, a thief broke into our house.*

Mood

Mood refers to the emotions an audience experiences as the result of the atmosphere created in a piece of writing or a media text.

SEE also **Atmosphere**

Narration/Narrative Writing

Narration relates one or more events in story form, usually in the order in which they happen. Narrative writing can be fictional or non-fictional.

Noun

A noun is a word that names a person, place, quality, thing, action, or idea; the underlined words in this sentence are nouns: *When Joe was at the library in Truro, curiosity enticed him to read an article that claimed fear could be cured by meditation.*

These are the five main types of nouns:

- abstract: *happiness, beauty, courage*
- concrete: *hand, birthday party, examination*

- collective: *class, herd, bunch*
- proper: *Janice, Edmonton, December, Acadia University, Canada Day* (Proper nouns identify a particular person, place, time, organization, or event, and always begin with a capital letter.)
- common: *girl, city, month, school, holiday* (The term common noun is used to refer to any noun that is not a proper noun.)

An *appositive* is a noun or a noun phrase that relates to or explains a noun or pronoun that immediately precedes it. Appositives are set off with commas:

I wrote to Amy Kim, <u>my best friend</u>.

Mr. Mohan, <u>the principal</u>, stood up.

Object

The English language has three types of objects. In the following examples, the direct object is underlined and the indirect object is in roman type.

- A *direct object* is a noun or pronoun that answers the question *what?* or *whom?* after the verb: *He bought a <u>kite</u>.*
- An *indirect object* answers the question *to what?, to whom?, for what?,* or *for whom?* relating to the verb: *He bought me a <u>kite</u>.*
- The *object of a preposition* is a noun or pronoun that comes at the end of a phrase that begins with a preposition: *He bought a <u>kite</u> for me.*

SEE also **Sentence**

Objective/Subjective

SEE **Point of View**

Paragraph

A paragraph is a group of sentences that develop one aspect of a topic, or one phase of a narrative. The sentences in a paragraph should have both unity and coherence. Sometimes, especially in essays, the aspect or point being developed is expressed in a topic sentence, and the other sentences in the paragraph expand on this statement.

SEE also **Unity**, **Coherence**, and **Topic Sentence**

Parallel Structure

Parallel structure in a sentence refers to two or more elements that are of equal importance and expressed in similar grammatical terms. Sentences without parallel structure can sound awkward and confusing. Parallel structure is often signalled by expressions such as *both … and, either … or, not only … but also,* and *whether … or.* Parallelism is especially important for the correct listing of items in a series. Parallel words, phrases, or clauses are typically joined by the conjunctions *and, but,* and *or.*

Not parallel: *Skateboarders are taught toe edging, heel edges, and how to switch.*

Parallel: *Skateboarders are taught toe edges, heel edges, and switches.*

or

Skateboarders are taught to toe edge, heel edge, and switch.

SEE also **Balance**

Paraphrase

A paraphrase is a restatement, in the writer's own words, of something the writer has read or heard. Paraphrasing allows writers to reduce the need for quotations when using source material. However, this source material must be properly cited in order to avoid plagiarism.

SEE also **Citation**, **Bibliography**, **Endnotes**, **Footnotes**, and **Plagiarism**

Parts of Speech

A part of speech is one of eight categories into which words are grouped according to their uses in a sentence.

SEE **Adjective**, **Adverb**, **Conjunction**, **Interjection**, **Noun**, **Preposition**, **Pronoun**, and **Verb**

Personal Response

A personal response is an exploration of a print or media text. It expresses the writer's feelings and thoughts about the text, and makes connections between the text and the writer's personal experiences and background knowledge.

SEE also **Critical Response**

Personification

Personification is a form of metaphor in which inanimate objects or ideas are given human characteristics. Example: *Bony fingers of ice along the edge of the roof pointed down at him accusingly.*

SEE also **Figurative Language/Figures of Speech** and **Metaphor**

Persuasion/Persuasive Writing

Persuasion is writing that tries to convince a reader of something. Persuasion is usually intended to influence or change people's opinions, beliefs, attitudes, choices, or behaviours.

Phrase

A phrase is a group of closely related words that does not contain a subject and a verb. A phrase can act as a noun, an adjective, or an adverb.

- A *noun phrase* acts as a noun: <u>To win the game</u> is the goal.
- An *adjective phrase* acts as an adjective: I prefer the shirt <u>with the blue stripes</u>.
- An *adverb phrase* acts as an adverb: Brendan spoke <u>for the first time</u>.

SEE also **Adjective**, **Adverb**, **Noun**, and **Clause**

Plagiarism

Plagiarism refers to using the exact words, ideas, or writing of someone else and presenting them as your own. Considered theft because a writer's property has been used without permission, plagiarism is a serious academic offence in schools, universities, and colleges.

SEE also **Citation, Bibliography**, **Endnotes**, **Footnotes**, and **Paraphrase**

Point of View

Point of view in writing can mean one of the following:

- The writer is mainly *objective* or *subjective* in presenting a topic. This usually applies to non-fiction writing such as news reports, research papers, personal essays, and opinion pieces. The writer of a research paper, for example, is expected to be objective, presenting ideas and information supported by accurate and reliable references that the reader can check. On the other hand, the writer of a personal essay or an opinion piece is subjective, presenting mainly her or his own thoughts and feelings about a topic.
- In a piece of fiction such as a short story or novel, the point of view is the perspective from which the story is told:
  - *First-person point of view* means that everything presented in the story is seen and interpreted from only one personal perspective, using the first-person pronoun.

– *Omniscient third-person point of view* allows the writer to tell the reader what all the characters are doing and thinking as the plot unfolds. When a writer uses a *limited omniscient point of view*, the story is also told in the third person, but from the perspective of only one character.

SEE also **Pronoun**

Predicate

A predicate is the part of a sentence that contains a verb and any objects and other related words or phrases. Each of the underlined examples below is a predicate.

They <u>arrived</u>.

They <u>arrived earlier than expected</u>.

Jason <u>is the best player</u>.

Sujata and Clifton <u>have been successful year after year</u>.

SEE also **Subject, Sentence, Object**, and **Phrase**

Preposition

A preposition is a word that shows the relationship between a noun or pronoun (called the object of the preposition) and some other word in the sentence. Many prepositions are single words, such as *at, about, above, against, between, by, during, for, from, in, on, of, out, to, since, toward,* and *with.* Some prepositions contain more than one word, for example: *according to, ahead of, because of, in addition to, in spite of,* and *instead of.*

A prepositional phrase begins with a preposition and ends with a noun or pronoun (the object of the preposition), and acts as an adjective, an adverb, or, less commonly, as a noun:

The books <u>in the library</u> are <u>for everyone</u>. (adjective phrases)

<u>On behalf of the group</u>, I accept your invitation <u>with great pleasure</u>. (adverb phrases)

<u>From my house to yours</u> is only three blocks. (noun phrase)

Pronoun

A pronoun is a word that replaces a noun or another pronoun: *<u>I</u> saw <u>it</u> on the horizon.* A *personal pronoun* refers to a person: *<u>He</u> is my <u>brother</u>.*

The *number* of a noun, pronoun, or verb shows whether it is singular (one thing) or plural (more than one thing):

• singular: *<u>She</u> <u>is</u> a happy <u>child</u>.*
• plural: *<u>They</u> <u>are</u> happy <u>children</u>.*

The *person* of a pronoun indicates whether someone is speaking (first person), is being spoken to (second person), or is being spoken about (third person). Personal pronouns and verbs change their forms to show person.

• first person: *<u>I listen</u> to music. <u>We listen</u> to music.*
• second person: *<u>You listen</u> to music.*
• third person: *<u>He/she listens</u> to music. <u>They listen</u> to music.*

Pronouns have subject and object cases, which can be singular or plural. See the following chart.

	Subject Case		Object Case		Possessive Case	
	Singular	Plural	Singular	Plural	Singular	Plural
First person	*I*	*we*	*me*	*us*	*my, mine*	*our, ours*
Second person	*you*	*you*	*you*	*you*	*your, yours*	*your, yours*
Third person	*he, she, it*	*they*	*him, her, it*	*them*	*his, her, hers, its*	*their, theirs*

SEE also **Pronoun Usage**

Pronoun Usage

Watch for the following pitfalls of pronoun usage:

- Noun/pronoun agreement requires that the writer make clear which word the pronoun is replacing (its antecedent). Here is an example of a pronoun with an unclear antecedent and how the sentence can be clarified:

  Unclear: *Linda loves looking after Sandy, because she is so good.*

  Clear: *Linda loves looking after Sandy, because Sandy is so good.*

- Personal pronouns should agree in number and gender with the noun or pronoun they replace.

  Incorrect: *A clown always looks happy, even if they are crying inside.*

  Correct: *Clowns always look happy, even if they are crying inside.*

  Be especially careful when using pronouns with reference to gender. The first example below is now generally considered unacceptable, but can be easily corrected by using the plural forms of the noun and pronoun.

  Sexist: *A clown always looks happy, even if he is crying inside.*

  Non-sexist: *Clowns always look happy, even if they are crying inside.*

  SEE also **Sexist/Non-sexist Language**

- Usually you will have no trouble choosing the right case of a personal pronoun. However, pay attention when the pronoun is joined to another noun or pronoun by *and, or,* or *nor.* Use the case of the pronoun that you would use if the other noun or pronoun were not there.

  Incorrect: *Neither Carlo nor me had done the work.*

  Correct: *Neither Carlo nor I had done the work.*

  Incorrect: *Ms. Jackson read the book to Fatima and I.*

  Correct: *Ms. Jackson read the book to Fatima and me.*

- When you use a personal pronoun immediately after a form of the verb *to be* (for example, *am, is, are, was, were, had been, will be*), you normally use the objective case in informal speech: *It's me.* However, in formal language, it is correct to use the subjective case: *It was I who did all the work.*

- Sometimes the pronouns *we* and *us* are used just before a noun. In sentences such as the following, check that you are using the correct case of the pronoun by reading the sentence without the following noun to see if it is correct.

  Incorrect: *Us dog owners love to talk about our pets.*

  Correct: *We dog owners love to talk about our pets.*

- Pronouns referring to a noun such as *team* or *group* can be singular or plural, depending on whether the emphasis is on the whole unit or on individual members.

  The team will make its best effort.

  The team will make their ways separately to the game.

SEE also **Antecedent**

Punctuation

Punctuation marks such as apostrophes, commas, semicolons, and periods are used to indicate relationships between words, phrases, and clauses.

Redundancy/Redundant

Redundancy is the use of unnecessary words in a sentence.

Redundant: *I woke up at 7:30 a.m. in the morning.*

Better: *I woke up at 7:30 a.m.*

Redundant: *The reason I stayed home is because I was sick.*

Better: *I stayed home because I was sick.*

Rhetorical Question

A rhetorical question is one asked for dramatic effect rather than to get information. It often serves to set up a point that the writer or speaker will address.

Does anyone care?

How long have we been waiting for solutions to this problem?

Isn't it obvious that she is the best choice for the position?

Run-on Sentence

A run-on sentence (sometimes called a *fused sentence*) is formed when two sentences are run into each other, which is an error. To fix a run-on sentence, either add the proper punctuation with perhaps a conjunction, or break the run-on sentence into two separate sentences.

Incorrect: *Mei Lin didn't like the decision she felt it was wrong.*

Correct: *Mei Lin didn't like the decision, because she felt it was wrong.*

Correct: *Mei Lin didn't like the decision. She felt it was wrong.*

Script

A script is the written text of a play, movie, or television drama. Scripts are made up of dialogue (the actors' spoken words) and stage directions.

Sentence

A sentence is a group of words expressing a complete thought. It contains a subject and predicate.

- A *simple sentence* consists of one principal, or independent, clause: *He entered the room.* There are five basic simple-sentence patterns:
  - subject-verb: *The dog barked.*
  - subject-verb-direct object: *The dog wanted a toy.*
  - subject-verb-indirect object-direct object: *Rajiv gave the dog the toy.*
  - subject-linking verb-adjective subject completion: *The dog was content.*
  - subject-linking verb-noun subject completion: *Rajiv was his hero.*
- A *compound sentence* consists of two or more principal clauses: *He entered the room and he sat down.*

- A *complex sentence* consists of one principal clause and one or more subordinate clauses: <u>*While I watched*</u>, *<u>he entered the room</u>.*
- A *compound-complex sentence* consists of two principal clauses and one or more subordinate clauses: *While I watched, he entered the room and then he sat down.*

SEE also **Subject**, **Predicate**, **Object**, and **Clause**

Sentence Fragment

A fragment is a piece of something. A sentence fragment is a piece of a sentence—not a complete sentence—and therefore an error. Sentence fragments are acceptable in dialogue, spoken English, and sometimes in informal writing, but are not appropriate in formal writing.

Fragment: *We went to the game on Saturday. <u>Just Josh and I</u>.* (lacks a verb)

Revised: *Just Josh and I went to the game on Saturday.*

Fragment: *Never did understand those engines.* (lacks a subject)

Revised: *I never did understand those engines.*

In certain circumstances, a sentence fragment may be purposely used for emphatic effect, but this should be done sparingly.

Sexist/Non-sexist Language

Sexist language is language that states or implies a gender stereotype, such as that all men are or should be leaders, or that all women are or should be sensitive and caring. The following are two sexist statements:

A good leader knows how to inspire his followers.

When a nurse comes, she will take care of you.

A common way to avoid sexist language is to use plural forms of nouns and pronouns:

Good leaders know how to inspire their followers.

Another way is to use *he or she,* although this should be done sparingly:

When a nurse comes, he or she will take care of you.

Alternatives are also available for traditional, non-inclusive words (for example, *chair* instead of *chairman,* *sales representative* instead of *salesman,* *firefighter* instead of *fireman,* *police officer* instead of *policeman,* and *worker* instead of *workman*).

Simile

A simile makes an explicit comparison between two things, using *like* or *as.*
The icicles, like bony fingers, hung from the edge of the roof.

SEE also **Figurative Language/Figures of Speech** and **Metaphor**

Slang

Slang is extremely informal language used in conversation, especially with friends. Slang is generally not acceptable in writing other than as quoted words or in dialogue.

SEE also **Formal/Informal Language**

Style

Style refers to the distinctive manner of a writer's or speaker's expression—how he or she writes or says what is written or said. Style is created mainly through diction, the use of figurative language, and the length and types of sentences included in spoken or written language.

SEE also **Diction**, **Figurative Language/Figures of Speech**, and **Sentence**

Subject

The subject of a sentence is the word (or phrase, or clause) that names the person, place, or thing about which something is said.

The doctor said that I need rest.

That group of friends has been together for years.

Whoever holds the winning ticket has not claimed the prize.

SEE also **Phrase** and **Clause**

Subject-Verb Agreement

A verb should always agree in number with its subject. This means that a singular subject takes a singular verb, and a plural subject takes a plural verb. Here are some tips:

- Prepositional phrases such as *at school, under my desk, through the woods, with great sadness,* and *of the cars* never contain the subject of a sentence.

  Incorrect: *One of the cars were stolen.* (*Cars* is not the subject.)

  Correct: *One of the cars was stolen.* (The singular verb *was* agrees with the singular subject *one.*)

- If the subject has two parts, joined by *or, not either ... or,* or *neither ... nor,* make the verb agree with the part of the subject nearest to it:

  Neither my brother nor my parents were at my concert.

  Neither my brothers nor my sister was at my concert.

- Some subjects look like they are plural, but they are really singular:

  The news is about to come on.

  Billiards is a popular game with that group.

SEE also **Subject** and **Phrase**

Summary

A summary is a shortened version, in a writer's own words, of a speech or a written source such as a news report, profile, or section of a textbook.

Syllable

A syllable is the part of a word that contains one vowel sound. For example:

- *idea* has three syllables (*i, e,* and *a* vowel sounds)
- *worked* has only one syllable (*o* vowel sound)

Symbol

A symbol is something that stands for or represents an idea or quality other than itself. Some widely known symbols are a maple leaf for Canada and a lion for courage. Symbols usually evoke strong feelings associated with the concept they represent.

Synonym

Synonyms are words that have the same, or almost the same, meaning. For example, the adjectives *slender, slim, lean, thin, skinny,* and *scrawny* all mean more or less the same thing, but each has a different connotation. While a dictionary or thesaurus will provide lists of synonyms, it's important to choose the word that conveys the writer's precise, intended meaning.

SEE also **Connotation/Denotation**

Syntax

Syntax is the arrangement of words to form sentences, clauses, or phrases. It is also referred to as sentence structure.

SEE also **Sentence, Clause,** and **Phrase**

Tense

SEE **Verb Tense**

Theme

The theme of a story is its unifying general observation about life or human nature.

Thesis/Thesis Statement

The thesis is the main idea of an essay. The thesis statement is the expression of that idea in a sentence.

Tone

Tone refers to the attitude of a writer toward a topic, as expressed in a piece of writing. Tone reveals how the writer feels about the subject and may also reveal his or her underlying values, attitudes, and beliefs. A tone can be humorous, serious, angry, proud, and so on. Tone is usually conveyed through diction, word connotations, and sentence length.

SEE also **Connotation/Denotation** and **Diction**

Topic Sentence

A topic sentence expresses the main idea in a paragraph.

Transitional Devices

Transitional devices are words or phrases that link ideas, sentences, or paragraphs, making it easier for the reader to understand how the parts of a paragraph or longer piece of writing are related to each other. Transitional devices include *however, in addition, most important, next, similarly,* and *in fact.*

SEE also **Coherence** and **Transition Sentence**

Transition Sentence

In a series of sequential paragraphs, often either the first or the last sentence of a paragraph acts as a transition sentence, creating coherence by connecting the ideas of that paragraph to the one coming either immediately before or after it.

SEE also **Coherence** and **Transitional Devices**

Unity

Unity occurs when all the parts of a piece of writing relate to a main idea (thesis). Unity is considered a principle of effective writing.

SEE also **Coherence** and **Thesis/Thesis Statement**

Verb

A verb is a word or phrase that expresses an action or a state of being.

The weather <u>was</u> fine all day.

I <u>will write</u> my essay this week.

There are several forms of verbs:

- A *helping verb* precedes its main verb. Common helping verbs are *be, do, have, can/could, may/might,* and *will.*
  She <u>can</u> help you.
  We <u>might</u> go.
- A *transitive verb* requires an object to complete its meaning: *We <u>value</u> your opinion.*
- An *intransitive verb* does not require an object to complete its meaning: *The sun <u>rises</u>.*
- A *linking verb* connects a subject with a complement: *The shirt <u>is</u> red.* The most common linking verb is a form of the verb *to be.*

SEE also **Subject-Verb Agreement**, **Verb Tense**, and **Voice**

Verb Tense

Verb tense refers to the time frame expressed by the form of a verb. English has nine main categories of tense:

- present: *they work*
- past: *they worked*
- future: *they will work*

- present perfect: *they have worked*
- past perfect: *they had worked*
- future perfect: *they will have worked*

- present progressive: *they are working*
- past progressive: *they were working*
- future progressive: *they will be working*

SEE also **Verb**

Voice

1 A verb is in the *active voice* if its subject is the doer of the action. A verb is in the *passive voice* when the subject of the verb receives the action.

Active: *The firefighters <u>extinguished</u> the fire.*

Passive: *The fire was extinguished <u>by the firefighters</u>.*

SEE also **Verb**

2 (writing trait) Voice is the distinctive style of a piece of writing, the expression of the writer's personality and individuality. Word choice, sentence structure, tone, and imagery contribute to the development of voice.

Works Cited

SEE **Bibliography**

Writing Process

Writing is a dynamic process in which writers engage to develop their ideas into polished written pieces. While no two writers follow the same steps or methods, the process for most formal writing usually involves the following: understanding the topic; understanding audience and purpose; brainstorming; focussing on a thesis; collecting and reviewing information; organizing information; writing a draft; revising; editing; proofreading; and publishing a final copy.

Index

Similar words, 18

Similes, 80

Slang, 3, 31, 59, 63, 160

Soliloquies, 87

Sources
documenting, 121–122, 124–127
evaluation of, 121
of research information, 118–121

Spacing, 65, 82

Special effects, in movies, 102

Speeches, 143–145

Spell-checkers, 5, 60, 177

Spelling, 62, 175–179. *See also*
Misspellings

Square brackets, 122, 186

Stage directions, 86–87

Stanzas, 81

Story ideas, 75

Subject–verb agreement, 62, 156

Subordinate clauses, 158

Subtopics, 26
in body paragraphs, 52
in brainstorming, 33, 34
lists grouped by, 41
order of, 26, 42
organizing information within,
44–46
in revision stage, 56
in thesis development, 36–37, 38
in writing for assessment, 151

Summaries, 111–112

Superscript, 124

T-charts, 35, 91

Thank-you letters, 141

Themes, of short stories, 75

Thesauruses, 58, 159, 163, 164

Thesis. *See also* Main idea
additional information to support,
39
focussing on, 25, 36–38
restatement of, 151

Thesis statement
in drafts, 50–51
in essays, 21, 25
in final *vs.* working form, 67

focus on topic and, 36
in opinion pieces, 113
revising, 38, 56
in writing for assessment, 150
in writing process, 25
in writing summaries, 111

Third person
in news reports, 107
point of view, 76

Time management, 192–194

Title page, 64–65

Titles of works of literature, 186, 188

Topic
focussing on, 29
understanding, 25, 29

Topic sentences, 13, 14, 52, 111, 150

Traits of writing, 2–5

Transitional devices, 4
and coherence, 18
commas with, 182
in concluding paragraph, 54
in first draft, 26
and parallel structure, 19
semicolons with, 186
for sentence variety, 58, 157
for smooth connections, 57
in writing for assessment, 151

Types of writing, 6–9

Underlining, 63

Unity, 13
in essays, 21
of paragraphs, 17–18

Unrhymed verses, 81

Verbs
in active voice, 161
in passive voice, 161
proofreading, 60
tenses, 62, 151, 156

Verses, 81

Visual aids
in oral presentations, 148
in speeches, 143–144

Visual materials, in books being
reviewed, 99

Vocabulary building, 164

Credits

Text Credits

Page 80: "The Streets of Purple Cloth" from *The Small Words in My Body* by Karen Connelly, published in *Grace and Poison* (Turnstone Press, 2001). Copyright © 1991 Karen Connelly. Reprinted with permission of the author. **Page 81:** "The Eel" © 1941 by Ogden Nash. Reprinted with permission of Curtis Brown, Ltd. **Page 81:** "Your Buildings" from *Poems of Rita Joe*, Abanaki Press, 1978. Copyright © The Estate of Rita Joe. Reprinted with permission. **Page 82:** "Progress" by Emma LaRocque, first published in *Canadian Literature: A Quarterly of Criticism and Review*, #124–125, Spring/Summer 1990. Copyright © Emma LaRocque. Reprinted with permission. **Pages 109–110:** "Timberlea teen helps, two shoes at a time" by Joel Jacobson, dated December 16, 2007. Reprinted with permission from the Halifax Herald Limited.

Cartoon Credits

Page 5: Frogs and Voice. Copyright © 2008—The Cartoon Bank. All rights reserved. **Page 26:** For Better or For Worse © Lynn Johnston Productions. 1989. Dist. by Universal Press Syndicate. Reprinted with permission. All rights reserved. **Page 38:** FOXTROT © Bill Amend. Reprinted with permission of Universal Press Syndicate. All rights reserved. **Page 117:** Copyright © 2008 by Sidney Harris. **Page 152:** FOXTROT © Bill Amend. Reprinted with permission of Universal Press Syndicate. All rights reserved. **Page 187:** HERMAN® is reprinted with permission from LaughingStock Licensing Inc., Ottawa, Canada. All rights reserved.